中国科学院大学
研究生教材系列

学科英语写作教程
电子工程

Writing a
Research Paper in
Electronics Engineering

总主编◎高　原　张红晖
主　编◎李　晰

清华大学出版社
北京

内 容 简 介

本教材共分为六章，编者选取 IEEE 期刊文章自建语料库，真实呈现期刊论文的体裁特征和语言规范。围绕 IEEE 期刊论文常见的 IMRD 结构展开，详细介绍了学术论文写作各个环节包含的步骤以及目的，同时也关注每个部分的常见语言点，辅以相应练习，助力学生提高学术论文写作能力。

本教材既可作为学术英语写作教材，也可作为学术论文写作的参考工具书。

版权所有，侵权必究。举报：010-62782989，beiqinquan@tup.tsinghua.edu.cn。

图书在版编目（CIP）数据

学科英语写作教程.电子工程/高原，张红晖总主编；李晰主编.—北京：清华大学出版社，2022.11
中国科学院大学研究生教材系列
ISBN 978-7-302-62091-4

Ⅰ.①学… Ⅱ.①高… ②张… ③李… Ⅲ.①电子技术—英语—写作—研究生—教材 Ⅳ.① H319.36

中国版本图书馆 CIP 数据核字（2022）第 197770 号

责任编辑：刘细珍
封面设计：李尘工作室
责任校对：王凤芝
责任印制：曹婉颖

出版发行：清华大学出版社
网　　址：http://www.tup.com.cn, http://www.wqbook.com
地　　址：北京清华大学学研大厦A座　　邮　编：100084
社 总 机：010-83470000　　邮　购：010-62786544
投稿与读者服务：010-62776969, c-service@tup.tsinghua.edu.cn
质量反馈：010-62772015, zhiliang@tup.tsinghua.edu.cn

印 装 者：三河市君旺印务有限公司
经　　销：全国新华书店
开　　本：185mm×260mm　　印　张：9　　字　数：194千字
版　　次：2022年12月第1版　　印　次：2022年12月第1次印刷
定　　价：55.00元

产品编号：091875-01

总　　序

2020年11月，教育部新文科建设工作组发布的《新文科建设宣言》指出："文科教育融合发展需要新文科。新科技和产业革命浪潮奔腾而至，社会问题日益综合化复杂化，应对新变化、解决复杂问题亟需跨学科专业的知识整合，推动融合发展是新文科建设的必然选择。进一步打破学科专业壁垒，推动文科专业之间深度融通、文科与理工农医交叉融合，融入现代信息技术赋能文科教育，实现自我的革故鼎新，新文科建设势在必行。"学科英语是外语学科和专业学科相互交叉、彼此融合的产物，符合国家"新文科"建设的时代愿景。开辟外语学科建设的全新思路，是当前外语教学改革的重要突破方向。

"中国科学院大学研究生教材系列"将切实满足特定专业学生群体的英语学习需求作为教材编写的重要依据，充分考虑到具体学习者群体的学习目标和学习诉求，具有以实际应用为导向的根本特质。该系列教材不仅关注教材编写前期的需求分析，同时重视教材试用阶段使用者的实际反馈，因为我们认为，直面使用者反馈是确定教材价值的关键一环，是重新审视学习者需求的宝贵机会，更是反复改进教材质量的可靠抓手。

"中国科学院大学研究生教材系列"融入现代信息技术，运用语料库的数据处理方法，整理归纳学科英语的语言特点和语篇特征。语料库方法可以十分客观快捷地捕捉学术语篇中的词汇、短语、搭配、语块、句子结构等语言层面的使用规律，正在成为学术和学科英语研究领域新近涌现的热点之一。然而，语料库技术运用于教材编写的尝试却寥寥无几，该系列教材无疑为语料库方法运用于教材编写做出了开创性的贡献。语料库的运用不仅能够呈现自然学术语境中真实的语言使用，更为重要的是，能够引导学习者建立适合自己微观研究方向的专业文献语料库，并将其作为未来学术生涯的开端以及追随学术生命成长过程的见证。学科英语语料库一方面可以成为研究者文献阅读经历不断累积的记录，另一方面也可能成为研究者写作不竭的灵感源泉和他们未来指导学生进行专业写作的宝贵财富。基于学科英语语料库的教材建设在"授人以鱼"的同时也在"授人以渔",而学习者也会因此获得"授人以渔"的能力。

我们正处在一个教育变革的时代。新的时代呼唤符合国家发展需求的教育理念和新颖实用的教学方法,同时也鼓励教师队伍努力探索新型的教材编写模式。"中国科学院大学研究生教材系列"积极响应时代的要求,是国家"新文科"建设指导思想下的勇敢尝试。

该系列教材的出版得到中国科学院大学教材出版中心资助,在此表示感谢。

高　原
2022 年 5 月

前　　言

《学科英语写作教程：电子工程》是以语料库为基础学习学术论文写作，帮助学生做好国际期刊论文发表准备的教材。本书以学术论文常用的 IMRD 结构为基础，每个章节都延伸出适用 IEEE 期刊的语步，帮助学生理解学术论文写作的各个部分以及整体框架，并熟练掌握学术论文中的一些体裁特征，使用符合 IEEE 期刊规范的结构和语言。

一、教材对象

本教材主要面向具备较好的英语基础、有学术论文发表需求的硕士和博士研究生，也适合想要提高学术论文写作技巧的研究人员。

二、教材特点

本教材选取丰富的期刊文章自建语料库，全方位为读者呈现学术论文写作的要点和特点。主要特色如下：

1. 本教材自建语料库，语料来自 IEEE 影响因子 5 以上的 11 种期刊，具体为 *Internet of Things, Transactions on Automatic Control, Transactions on Automation Science and Engineering, Transactions on Communications, Transactions on Circuits and Systems for Video Technology, Transactions on Geoscience and Remote Sensing, Transactions on Mobile Computing, Transactions on Multimedia, Transactions on Pattern Analysis and Machine Intelligence, Transactions on Vehicular Technology*，*Computational Intelligence Magazine*，均为这些期刊中的高被引文章或者 2016 年以后发表的文章，共计 87 篇，约 55 万字。

2. 本教材所选语料的体例和格式也都保留了期刊论文的特点，目的是尽可能让读者熟悉真实的学术论文结构和语言特点。

3. 本教材强调学术论文的体裁特征和规范，详尽地展示了论文写作整体框架和各个部分的语言特征。

三、内容安排

本教材以 Introduction, Method, Results 和 Discussion 为基本结构，详细描述了每个部分展开的步骤以及相关的语言要点。同时，本教材配有丰富的练习，方便读者在每个单元的学习之后及时练习。

全书以 IMRD 基本结构为主线，每个部分按照数个不同 Move（语步）展开，详细解释了每个语步分别包括哪些步骤，以及其在论文中的作用和目的。同时，还针对有些期刊的结构，介绍了文献综述以及摘要的写法，帮助学生更好地理解这几个部分的写作。

本书每个语步和步骤都辅以丰富的例证，供学生模仿借鉴。同时，每个单元都以语步为单位，设几个 Language Focus（语言要点），重点关注有关部分需要注意的语言特征，如被动语态、v-ing 表因果关系等，让学生能够意识到，针对学术论文写作的不同部分，我们也应该使用相应的语言技巧。另外，每个单元设有练习，练习本单元相应的语步和语言点。

本教材是编者在近年教学实践基础上的经验积累和突破。编者水平有限，时间仓促，书中难免会有错误和不足之处，欢迎读者朋友们批评指正。

编 者
2022 年 6 月

Contents

Chapter 1 Building an IEEE Journal Corpus 1

    1.1 Lead-in   2
    1.2 Coding   2

Chapter 2 Introducing Background 9

    2.1 Lead-in   10
    2.2 Establishing a Research Territory   12
    2.3 Establishing a Niche   19
    2.4 Occupying the Niche   25
    2.5 Stating the Outline of the Article   29

Chapter 3 Describing Methods 37

    3.1 Lead-in   38
    3.2 Contextualizing Study Methods   39
    3.3 Describing the Study   45
    3.4 Establishing Credibility   49
    3.5 Figure Description   50
    3.6 Language Focus   57

Chapter 4 Reporting Results 61

    4.1 Lead-in   62
    4.2 Contextualizing Results   63

    4.3 Reporting Results   69

    4.4 Summarizing Results   75

    4.5 Language Focus   77

Chapter 5   Discussing Findings   91

    5.1 Lead-in   92

    5.2 Revisiting Previous Sections   93

    5.3 Consolidating Results   97

    5.4 Stating Limitations and Future Research   104

    5.5 Language Focus   108

Chapter 6   Writing Abstract   113

    6.1 Lead-in   114

    6.2 Introducing Research Topic   115

    6.3 Describing the Research Method   117

    6.4 Summarizing the Research Results   118

    6.5 Presenting the Research Conclusions   120

References   123

Keys to Exercises   125

Chapter 1
Building an IEEE Journal Corpus

1.1 Lead-in

Corpus can be used as a computer-based tool for description of language, and enables analysis of a certain scope of language (Bieber, 1993). For example, a subject-specific corpus would help analyze the styles of language use in a particular subject.

For this textbook, a corpus of about 550,000 words gathered from 87 articles published during 2016—2021 in 11 IEEE (Institute of Electrical and Electronic Engineers) journals is built for the analysis of rhetorical moves and steps within each section of a research article as well as the specific language styles used accordingly. These articles were selected from journals on different topics. It should be admitted that the average selection of 8 articles per journal may not be able to fully present the variations of rhetorical moves and language styles. However, the corpus is well managed in terms of representativeness through the following criteria:

(1) The journals are with impact factors above 5, i.e. *Internet of Things, Transactions on Automatic Control, Transactions on Automation Science and Engineering, Transactions on Communications, Transactions on Geoscience and Remote Sensing, Transactions on Circuits and Systems for Video Technology, Transactions on Mobile Computing, Transactions on Multimedia, Transactions on Pattern Analysis and Machine Intelligence, Transactions on Vehicular Technology, Computational Intelligence Magazine*, and they cover a wide spectrum of topics within IEEE field;

(2) The articles are either highly cited or newly published (within three years);

(3) The articles contain four basic sections: Introduction, Methods, Results and Discussion;

(4) The articles are written by native English speakers;

(5) The articles are selected based on academic rigor, high-quality writing and clear presentation.

It is notable that the corpus is open to new articles from different journals.

1.2 Coding

After data collection, we can convert the articles into plain text and then proceed to data coding. Coding consists of two phases: One is manual annotation of moves and steps, and the other is automatic semantic tagging of words with a parser.

 ### 1.2.1 Move Coding

Based on the functional segments of a text, different Moves and Steps in the four main sections are identified, as shown in the following table:

Table 1.1 Moves and Steps in a research article

Sections	Moves	Steps
Introduction	Establishing a research territory	Claiming the centrality
		Making topic generalization(s)
		Reviewing items of previous research
	Establishing the niche	Counter-claiming
		Indicating a research gap
		Question-raising
		Continuing a tradition
	Occupying the niche	The purpose of the current research
		The main features of the current research
		Stating the outline of the article
Methods	Contextualizing the study methods	Stating the purpose of the methods
		Referencing previous works
		Identifying the methodological approaches
	Describing the study	Rationalizing the methods
		Describing the data
		Describing experimental/study procedures
	Establishing credibility	
Results	Contextualizing results	Providing background information
		Listing procedures or methodological techniques
		Stating research questions or hypothesis
		Describing aims and purposes
		Referring to previous research
		Summarizing main results
	Reporting results	Showing results by figures or tables
	Summarizing results	Instantiating results
		Invalidating results

(Continued)

Sections	Moves	Steps
Discussion	Revisiting previous sections	Revisiting the Introduction
		Revisiting the Methodology
		Revisiting the Results
	Consolidating results	Reporting results
		Comparing results
		Evaluating results
	Stating limitations and future research	

To annotate the data, we need to use a corpus tool, UAM Corpus Tool. It is developed by Mick O'Donell and is easy to use. You can download it for free from the UAM Corpus Tool website.

First, we can click "Start New Project" (Figure.1.1), and name our new project "IEEE project".

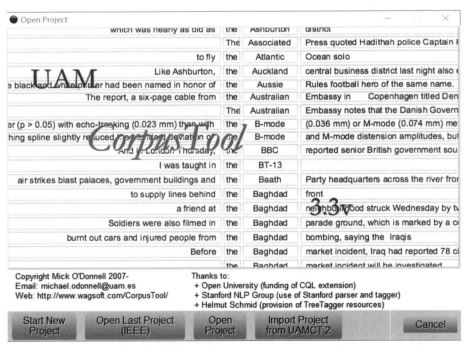

Figure 1.1 Start a new project in UAM Corpus Tool

Second, before we extend our corpus, we can chunk all the articles in sections (i.e., Introduction, Methods, Results and Discussion), and save them into separate plain text files. Then, we can add files to our corpus, and incorporate them all at once or one by one (Figure.1.2).

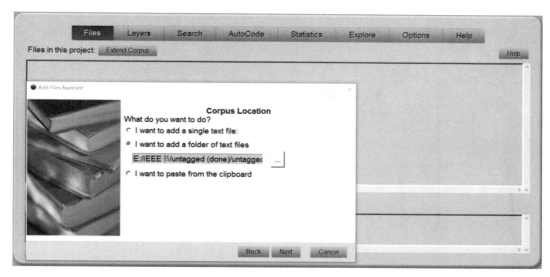

Figure 1.2 Add files to your corpus

Third, we need to add layers to our files (Figure.1.3). We can name the first layer "Moves", and a second layer "Steps" for further annotation.

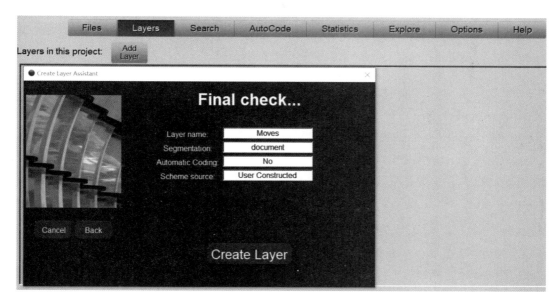

Figure 1.3 Add layers to your files

Fourth, we can create a system for our annotation. Choose the "Manual Annotation" type, and "Design your own scheme", and do not auto-segment the text (Figure.1.4).

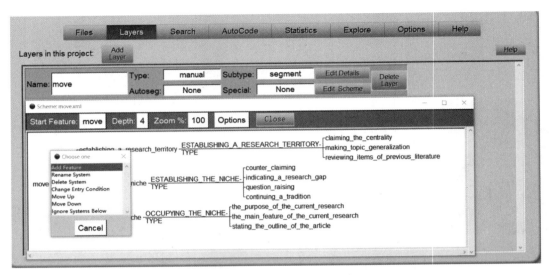

Figure 1.4 Design your own scheme

Then, by right clicking to add systems and features to the tree structure, we can get a system of Moves and Steps for Introduction.

After building up layers of moves and steps, we can get back to "Files" view, and select the paragraphs and sentences by clicking the bottom buttons to annotate the file (Figure.1.5). Once the annotation is done, we can use the files for further analysis.

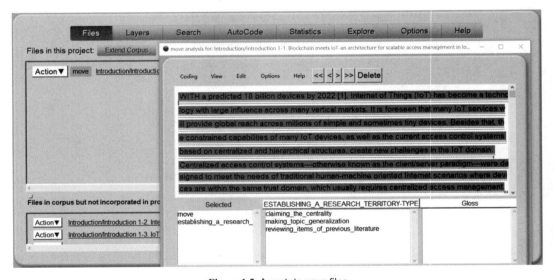

Figure 1.5 Annotate your files

For further introduction of UAM Corpus Tool, you can get detailed instructions from the homepage of the UAM Corpus Tool website.

1.2.2 Semantic Coding

We also need to tag the texts semantically. We can do this by adding another layer (Figure.1.6). First, click automatic annotation, and give our layer a name "POS", and then choose "Part of Speech (POS)", and then "Stanford Tagger". After that, the texts can be automatically annotated.

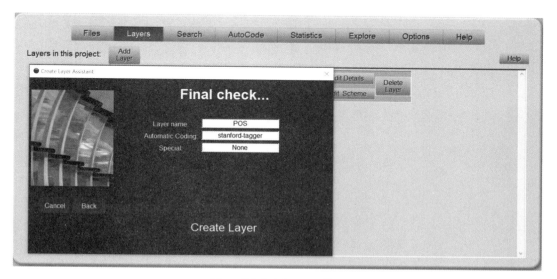

Figure 1.6 Autotag your files

Now, we have built a corpus of our own, which is ready for further analysis.

You can also use AntConc, a free concordance program (you can download it for free from Lawrence Anthony's Website) to analyze your data.

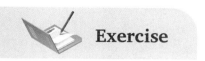

Exercise

Try to build your own corpus according to what you have learned in this chapter.

Chapter 2
Introducing Background

2.1 Lead-in

Read the following figure of doing a research and answer the following questions.

1. What parts in the figure do you think should be included in the Introduction of a research article?

2. What work should you do when doing background research?

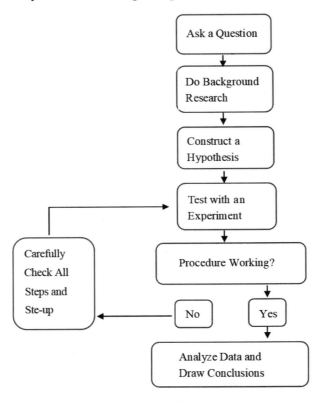

Figure 2.1 Research process (retrieved from Science Buddies Organization website)

An Introduction serves as the beginning of a research article. It is a guide for readers to quickly overview the research field as well as grasp the main content of the current research.

An Introduction is important in that you should tell a story about your research and get readers' attention by presenting them with the latest research trends and telling them how you manage to solve the problems that can expand the research field. To tell a good story, there are some tactics to use. No matter what the subject of research is, an Introduction usually consists of the following parts:

- establishing the context of the topic;
- reviewing the previous literature;
- indicating the research gap;
- stating the importance/purpose of the current research.

The patterns of an Introduction have been identified by different research, among which Toulmin's (1972) and Zappen's (1983) problem-solution model and Swales' (1990) CARS (Create a Research Space) model are the most cited. In this book, the latter is adopted. Swales (1990) identifies three basic rhetorical Moves in an Introduction:

- **Move 1: Establishing a research territory**

    Step 1 Claiming the centrality and/or

    Step 2 Making topic generalization(s) and/or

    Step 3 Reviewing items of previous research

- **Move 2: Establishing a niche**

    Step 1A Counter-claiming or

    Step 1B Indicating a research gap or

    Step 1C Question-raising or

    Step 1D Continuing a tradition

- **Move 3: Occupying the niche**

    Step 1A Outlining purposes or

    Step 1B Announcing present research

    Step 2 Announcing principal findings

    Step 3 Indicating the article's structure (optional)

Within each Move, a few obligatory and optional moves can be adopted to guide the structure of an Introduction.

In a word, in an Introduction, you need to tell the reader: What field your research is in, what topic you are focusing on, and why this topic is important. Sometimes, you can also briefly introduce how your research is conducted and how the article is organized.

2.2 Establishing a Research Territory

In the first part of an Introduction, you need to establish a research territory, which is the area that your research belongs to. You need to justify that your research is part of a significant research area by defining the topic, stating the specific problem to be addressed, and explaining why the problem is of interest/importance.

2.2.1 Claiming the Centrality

This very first step is a claim that appeals to the research community to accept the research to be reported as part of a lively, significant or well-established research area (Swales, 1990). We can begin with the definition of a topic or the general research area. Take the following paragraph as an example:

Excerpt	Comment
① Simultaneous localization and mapping (SLAM) and visual odometry (VO) are fundamental building blocks for many emerging technologies—from autonomous cars and UAVs to virtual and augmented reality. ② Realtime methods for SLAM and VO have made significant progress in recent years. ③ While for a long time the field was dominated by feature-based(indirect) methods, in recent years a number of different approaches have gained in popularity, namely direct and dense formulations.	The authors begin with the introduction of two terms (SLAM and VO) that specify the research in a certain field, that is, from autonomous cars and UAVs to virtual and augmented reality. This direct location of the research gives readers a clear direction of the research area. Then, the authors point out the progress made in these two technologies by reviewing the previous methods and introducing the new approaches in recent years.

(Engel, J., Koltun, V. & Cremers, D. 2017. Direct sparse odometry. *IEEE Transactions on Pattern Analysis and Machine Intelligence, 40(3)*: 611–625.)

This is the first paragraph of an Introduction of an IEEE research paper. It uses only three sentences to establish the research context for this paper. Readers can assume that the following would review the previous methods used for SLAM and VO, and then emphasize the current approaches. In fact, the paper continues to compare and contrast different approaches and explains what method is proposed in this paper.

The centrality claim can also include interest or importance, or claim that the research area is active by referring to other investigators (Swale, 1990). The first kind is more common, for example:

Excerpt	Comment
① Unmanned aerial vehicles (UAVs) are increasingly being used for intelligence, defense, and civilian information gathering and monitoring. ② This is particularly due to their utility in high endurance and perilous environments that are—as characterized by—dull, dirty, and dangerous. ③ A popular application of UAVs is information collection via surveillance of an area of operations. ④ Often, a fleet of UAVs is dispatched for large geographical coverage and multiple intelligence, surveillance, and reconnaissance (ISR) missions where the goal is to maximize the amount of information collected, and this results in the problem of routing and coordination.	This article begins with *X is increasingly being used for Y*. *X* is a specific research topic that is going to be conducted in the article, while *Y* usually refers to some general fields. This sentence claims the importance of *X* in different areas and its wide application, indicating huge potential research significance. Then, the focus moves from some general areas to a specific research area (i.e., "information collection via surveillance of an area of operations") in Sentence ③, thus introducing the research problem in the article, that is "the problem of routing and coordination" in Sentence ④.

(Thakoor, O., Garg, J. & Nagi, R. 2019. Multiagent UAV routing: A game theory analysis with tight price of anarchy bounds. *IEEE Transactions on Automation Science and Engineering, 17(1)*: 100–116.)

The first paragraph states clearly what we are going to study, and we should also make this topic seem interesting to the readers. The common sentence patterns used to begin an Introduction are shown below:

> * *X has been defined in [reference] as...*
> * *X is an interesting...scheme for future...because it has...*
> * *X has been technically challenged by exponentially increasing demands for...*
> * *X and Y play a key role in...*
> * *X will increase sevenfold between 2016 and 2021, reaching...by the end of 2021, and Y will account for over 80% of the total X.*
> * *In the last years, X has suffered an exponential growth, supported by the increasing popularity of Y, such as...*

> * *The increasing request for X motivates both academia and industry to invest in alternative solutions. X and Y were originally introduced about 60 years ago in Russia [reference]. Their exceptional robustness and good computational efficiency have immediately gained them much interest and many advocates in the...community.*
> * *X is considered to be indispensable for Y providing a wide variety of inherent features such as...*
> * *The development and growth of X in the past decade has led to the rapid adoption of Y and Z for...*

2.2.2 Making Topic Generalization(s)

This step "expresses in general terms the current state of the art of knowledge, of technique, or ... of current requirements for further progress" (Swales, 1990, p. 146). Note that the Step 1 and Step 2 are not always in a sequence and sometimes they overlap.

Excerpt	Comment
① Learning from data is essential to every area of science. ② It is the core of statistics and artificial intelligence, and is becoming ever more prevalent also in the engineering domain. ③ Control engineering is one of the domains where learning from data is now considered as a prime issue.	This paragraph develops from general to specific, beginning with a topic generalization sentence. Then, more details about the phenomena are added in Sentence ②. Sentence ③ narrows down the topic, and emphasizes the importance of leaning from data, which sets a foundation for further elaboration on this topic.

(De Persis, C. & Tesi, P. 2019. Formulas for data-driven control: Stabilization, optimality, and robustness. *IEEE Transactions on Automatic Control, 65(3)*: 909–924.)

Generally, the first paragraph begins with a statement about "knowledge or practice", or statement about "phenomena" (Swales, 1990, p. 146). Here, the sentence pattern *X (a research subject) is adj. to Y (an area)* is adopted to describe a phenomenon about learning from data, which is the topic of the research.

Here are more sentence patterns to make topic generalization(s):

> * *With..., X has become a technology with large influence across many fields.*
> * *X not only offers improvements in..., but also greatly improves..., including...*
> * *X is...(attribute) with...(another attribute). Its continuous operation leads to...*
> * *The benefits of X are understood across industries, with...(different industries).*
> * *X is one of the major developments of this paradigm, where...*
> * *A major development of X was the introduction of Y.*

> * Although it is common to study problems in which..., there are scenarios in which...
> * X can be seen as a typical case of Y and Z. These systems (i.e., Y and Z) can be decomposed into...and...
> * A significant amount of research effort has been devoted to X to enhance...
> * X is a...(attribute) that has shown good performance for solving difficult, time-critical problems when compared to other...methods, notably...
> * Recent advances in...have enabled the development of X.

2.2.3 Reviewing Items of Previous Research

Reviewing items of previous research is obligatory in almost every research article. As we all know, every research is closely related to the previous ones, either as a development or as a rebuttal of the previous research. Thus, literature review is a non-negligible part of a research paper.

A comprehensive literature review reveals the authors' ability in understanding the general field and synthesizing the previous literature to support their research. In some research papers, literature review is a subsection of the Introduction, while in some other papers, it can serve as a separate section. Wherever the literature review part is, its function is to introduce the state-of-the-art technologies/research on the topic, and it basically follows the similar structure and uses the similar sentence patterns. Through the review, the authors can justify their research by pointing out the weakness or research gap of the previous research.

Excerpt	Comment
① Considerable research has been undertaken on load balancing in a homogeneous wireless network, such as [9] and [10]. ② On the contrary, few studies have been done with respect to a hybrid Li-Fi and Wi-Fi network, and those few treat heterogeneous APs in the same way as in a homogeneous network. ③ In [11], a distributed load balancing method was proposed based on game theory, which requires quantities of iterations to reach a steady state. ④ With the aim of maximizing the overall throughput, [12] reported a centralized optimization method, which requires extensive computational complexity. ⑤ Those methods were developed from the APS solutions in a homogeneous network, and they fail to exploit the distinguishing characteristics between Li-Fi and Wi-Fi.	The review begins with a brief summary. Sentence ② then points out the few studies relevant to the current research. In the following sentences ③ and ④, specific methods used in previous research are introduced, followed by an inference made from the previous methods.

(Wu, X., Safari, M. & Haas, H. 2017. Access point selection for hybrid Li-Fi and Wi-Fi networks. *IEEE Transactions on Communications*, *65(12)*: 5375–5385.)

The structure of this literature review part can be simplified as: *Considerable research has been undertaken on X (a specific field). On the contrary, few studies have been done with respect to Y (another specific field). In [reference], there were details about X. [reference] reported more details. The previous mentioned methods fail to reach Y.*

The above paragraph is a clear example of reviewing previous literature. Its purpose is clear—to provide a method that can solve the problem Y. It begins with "Considerable research has been undertaken on..." Some examples of similar expressions are shown below. X stands for the research subject/topic, and Y stands for the research area or application.

* *X has been conducted in Y.*
* *X has already been studied from several points of view.*
* *X has long been studied in Y.*
* *X has been investigated for decades in Y.*
* *X as Y has been suggested and explored by many.*
* *There has been extensive research on X.*
* *Many X have been proposed in literature, usually in Y.*
* *X is a topic that has been studied in much detail in the research literature in the past and extensive reviews exist.*

The above expressions are usually used in the beginning of the literature review part. They serve to introduce the general research on this field but do not provide enough details for further elaboration. Then, the review part continues to introduce different perspectives on the research topic as well as to explore the potential weaknesses or problems the previous works have.

2.2.4 Language Focus

In literature review, citations are an indispensable part. They are central to persuasion, as they permit writers to engage in dialogue with source texts; provide justification and evidence for arguments and claims; demonstrate familiarity with the literature; show (dis)alignment with particular scholarship; and establish credibility (Hyland, 1999).

You might have noticed that in the above examples, there are different ways of intext citation: author-prominent and information-prominent. An author prominent citation is in the form of *author (year)+claim* (e.g., "Kingma et al. [14]① *take a similar view of dropout...*"), while an information-prominent citation is in the form of *claim+author (year)* (e.g., "*Industrial environments contain many hazardous areas that could benefit from robot assistance. Mining*

---

① This is the original reference in the cited article, and its form differs according to the specific journal.

operations [12] and structure inspection [13] are two such environments."). Note that "*Dropout was introduced by Srivastava et al. [3]*" is also an author-prominent citation.

Based on the corpus used in this book, we can tell that more information-prominent citations are used than author-prominent ones. In the corpus, the Introduction part has all together 1,165 citations. Citations account for 16.2 words per 1,000 words. Only 6% of the citations are author-prominent. This is because when reviewing literature, we are not just listing what have been done by whom, instead, we need to synthesize what we have read and present them in an organized way. Information-prominent citations are usually used to support a particular point, or deal with information that is not controversial. When we develop our own claims, we tend to use those information-prominent citations to make our claim solid and convincing. On the other hand, author-prominent citations are used for those ideas that we wish to emphasize the author(s), or to explore in detail, or to make compare and contrast. Hence, more citations are used in supporting sentences rather than used in claims. "Citation in the hard disciplines is therefore a means of integrating new claims into current knowledge while drawing on it as supporting testimony, situating the new work in the scaffolding of already accredited facts" (Hyland, 1999, p. 354).

Here are some examples of author-prominent citations:

* *For...systems, there is actually a fundamental result, which answers this question, proposed by AUTHORS [reference]. Initial work for...was developed by AUTHORS [reference].*
* *This strategy has been recently extended by AUTHORS [reference].*
* *The earliest work focused on..., ...and...of...was by AUTHORS [reference].*
* *AUTHORS [reference] discussed necessary and sufficient conditions under which...could be successful without being detected.*
* *AUTHORS [reference] designed a...that balances...and...for...*
* *AUTHORS [reference] have shown that their...effectively combines the positive properties of...and...approaches, producing...solutions independent of...*
* *Measurements by AUTHORS showed that better...was obtained for...than for... [reference], due to...*
* *AUTHORS performed wide...studies in the..., ..., and...GHz bands in..., and measurements showed significant signal attenuation (as great as...dB) due to...[reference].*
* *AUTHORS [reference] proposed a generic model of...*
* *AUTHORS [reference] defined the...as..., and then matched them through a...process.*
* *AUTHORS [reference] presented a...method that first applies...to..., then performs..., and finally...are aligned by...*
* *AUTHORS [reference] suggested to use...for..., by also incorporating a probabilistic measure to ensure robustness against...*

* AUTHORS [reference] also followed a...representation of..., before matching them.
* AUTHORS [reference] extended their previous approach in...problem [reference], to the case of...
* AUTHORS [reference] employ an approximated...specified interactively by the users while the more recent... [reference] system uses...and...to...
* The method introduced by AUTHORS [reference] interprets...through a...model that accounts for...in addition to..., and assumes that...
* AUTHORS [reference] demonstrate that, within their...framework, ...is the most informative feature while other features contribute complementary information.
* AUTHORS [reference] estimate...by applying a...function, before applying...prior [reference], refined iteratively by...as a post-processing step.
* AUTHORS [reference] introduce a...that is specific to...
* Both AUTHORS [reference] and AUTHORS [reference] used a...model with assumed known...index to estimate...from...
* AUTHORS [reference] took a similar approach but used a specular...model suitable for...
* AUTHORS [reference] also assumed...to disambiguate...; however, their approach can also estimate...
* As in our proposed method, AUTHORS [reference] exploited this via...
* Recently, AUTHORS [reference] derived constraints that allowed..., ...and...to be estimated from...under...(condition).
* AUTHORS [reference] combine...with...from...and resolve ambiguities via a...process.
* AUTHORS [reference] state that "...".
* AUTHORS [reference] conducted experiments showing that...
* AUTHORS [reference] improve...by building an approximate nearest neighbor graph.
* AUTHORS [reference] build a visual representation for...while generating...
* The work of...(year) of AUTHORS [reference] still provides a good frame of reference for reviewing the literature, describing methodologies on..., features and data association for general purposes.

According to Hyland (1999), citations are incorporated into the articles as a quotation, summary or generalization from several sources. Various reporting verbs are used in these sentences. In the corpus of this book, the most used 10 reporting verbs are: *state, provide, show, propose, present, develop, consider, describe, estimate, evaluate*.

In a word, before writing up a research article, we must have read a large quantity of relevant literature. As to the way we synthesize and present the literature to our reader, we have to be very familiar with the research topic and be able to use the literature to develop and refine our argument. To make an article profound and the argument convincing from the beginning to the end, sometimes, we can present part of the literature review in the Introduction, and leave the other parts in the Discussion to support our conclusion. The length of literature review varies according to the purpose of the review. As mentioned before, some articles have a dedicated section for literature review, which introduces the previous works critically and elaborates their relationship with the current research.

2.3 Establishing a Niche

The purpose of this move is to locate our research in a broad research field, so that our contribution can be foregrounded and evaluated. Through reading the previous research, we can find what have been done, how they are done, how they can be improved, and what has yet to be done, then we can develop our own research questions/hypothesis from the findings and create our own research space. This is called "establishing a niche". This step can be realized in different ways: (1) counter-claiming; (2) indicating a gap; (3) question raising; (4) continuing a tradition (Swales, 1990, p. 141).

2.3.1 Counter-claiming

We can make a counterclaim that the previous work has not covered a certain research topic, or has some limitations, by using "negative or quasi-negative quantifiers", "lexical negation", or "negation in the verb phrase" (Swales, 1990, p. 155).

Negative or quasi-negative quantifiers include *no*, *little*, *none*, *few*, *neither...nor*, etc. In the corpus, we can find the following instances of these quantifiers:

> * To the authors' best acknowledge, so far there has been <u>no</u> method specially tailored for...
> * To the best of our knowledge, <u>no</u> result is known for...with the total value function we consider in this paper.
> * However, ...are not interpretable and have <u>little</u> connection to...This is a limitation for...
> * While...offers a great opportunity to increase capacity, <u>little</u> is known about the...characteristics for...networks in...environments at these carrier frequencies.
> * Although...and...have been investigated under various...operations and...models for the past...years, the same problem under...<u>has not been</u> thoroughly analyzed even for the simplest...model.
> * However, traditional techniques <u>cannot</u> still match...

* After the development of the best analytical solution, <u>little</u> improvement in...was achieved until the advent of...
* To date, <u>few</u> studies have been carried out to investigate..., and those <u>few</u> are focused on...
* Aside from work conducted by authors at...University, there have been relatively <u>few</u> published...studies at...bands in...environments for...and...
* On the contrary, <u>few</u> studies have been done with respect to...
* Although the limitations to...are well known, <u>few</u> works propose...methods, of which...are examples, but often requiring additional assumptions.
* There are <u>few</u> studies that have considered...in their analysis.

Lexical negation means direct negation without any quantifier but with the use of some words, like verbs (*fail, lack*), adjectives (*inconclusive, misleading, limited, questionable, unable*), nouns (*lack, failure, limitation*), etc.

* A...may take a detailed assumption of..., but then may <u>fail</u> on an articulated object.
* However, the above methods <u>fail</u> to consider...caused by...
* Further, ...uses an extremely wide RF bandwidth, which may <u>limit</u> its application to...and...applications.
* Developing...is an ill-posed problem due to <u>lack</u> of information about...and...
* We showed that, in guaranteeing..., ...constraints can <u>limit</u>...
* While..., these...systems are <u>limited</u> to...This <u>limitation</u> can cause...when...and consequently affect...
* Despite their valuable achievements, these strategies <u>suffer</u> from a number of issues that <u>reduce</u> their practical applicability.
* However, ...has largely been <u>ignored</u> in...and...analysis.
* However, ...methodologies are known to be <u>undesirable</u> in the context of..., as they are not...and cannot easily incorporate..., ..., and...of...
* However, ...and...are often <u>unknown</u> in practice, implying...may require...
* With current mobile network designs, such required flexibility and elasticity are <u>hard</u> to realize, particularly due to the traditional usage of...that can neither dynamically...nor be easily upgraded with new functions.
* However, existing...methods mostly work on...task <u>solely</u> [reference], <u>without</u> exploiting...for...
* However, the performance of the existing...will <u>degrade</u> for...since it assumes...
* However, ...may <u>deteriorate</u> the...performance, and therefore it is important to find the optimal trade-off between...and..., which can be cast as a...problem.
* The fundamental problem of finding a...remains <u>challenging</u>.

Negation in the verb phrase refers to the use of *not* or some other adverbs like *rarely*, *seldom*, etc.

> * *For these reasons, traditional solutions building on...techniques are not affordable (because of...reasons) or simply impossible (when...is not known).*
> * *However, this might not be a valid assumption for..., where it is most likely for...to have..., both from...*
> * *The goal of meeting the desired service guarantees need to consider...aspects, as a...network will likely not be able to meet the service required by...*
> * *The...most commonly used in...does indeed enforce the creation of..., but the other defining properties of...do not seem to be explicitly enforced by the commonly used...*

2.3.2 Indicating a Research Gap

A research gap, in other words, what has not been done by the previous research, motivates us to do the current research. For the following parts of the article, we need to elaborate on how we would fill the gap, why our research is important and what contribution it will make to the field. Indicating a research gap can be realized by counter-claiming. The sentences we can use to identify the gap are:

> * *However, ...has been ignored by previous...methods, which limits their...abilities under...*
> * *However, to the best of our knowledge, ...for...has not been analyzed.*
> * *Understanding the impact of...on...and...of...systems, however, has not yet been considered.*
> * *The technique is simple, however, ...is marginally inaccurate. Notably, none of the methods [reference] solve the...issue.*
> * *Nevertheless, none of these studies has considered...and has mainly assumed...with hypothetical moments for...*
> * *Note that, apart from [reference], none of the previously mentioned works includes...and...in their modeling.*

2.3.3 Question-raising

By reviewing previous literature, we can identify the question to be answered or the problem to be solved, and then establish the niche.

> * *A main question is how to design...systems directly from...Besides their theoretical value, answers to this question could have a major practical impact especially in those situations where...can be difficult and time-consuming.*

* *A central question in...is how to replace...model with data.*
* *While the former problem has the optimal outcome, it is unclear as to...due to...This paper provides an answer to this question.*
* *...is a fundamental problem in...systems that requires...to...*
* *We believe that...is still not a solved problem and would like to highlight some of the challenges briefly.*
* *The design of a...that achieves such goal in this...market is still an open problem.*
* *In...and...research, it is an open problem to...*
* *A classical problem here is to maximize the probability of detecting a hidden target.*
* *However, the fundamental problem of finding...remains challenging.*

2.3.4 Continuing a Tradition

Some research niches are established by extending the previous work or making a few adjustments.

* *However, these studies assumed..., whereas in actual situations, ...always appear.*
* *The main focus in the above-mentioned studies, e.g. [reference], however, is on... Despite its relevance and importance, to the best of our knowledge, ...has not been fully investigated.*
* *The...performance can be further improved by using...approach.*
* *We build on results from related disciplines and extend existing techniques in various directions.*
* *This paper extends [reference] with three main contributions.*
* *Even though much research in this field has already been done, the original approach proposed in [reference] is still very popular. Therefore, in this paper, we extend the results of [reference] in order to obtain..., and to ensure...system without...*
* *It is possible to extend the...techniques developed in [reference] to...scenarios.*
* *In contrast to existing approaches, our method further takes full advantage of..., including..., ..., and...*

Although Move 2 takes only a couple of sentences in an Introduction, it's not insignificant. With the research niche clearly stated, we can create a research space that our readers can precisely identify. The niche also determines how we would develop our research question/hypothesis, which makes the essential part of our research and reflects our originality and innovativeness.

Chapter 2
Introducing Background

Excerpt	Comment
The Internet of Things (IoT) is a recent communication paradigm that envisions a near future, in which the objects of everyday life will be equipped with microcontrollers, transceivers for digital communication, and suitable protocol stacks that will make them able to communicate with one another and with the users, becoming an integral part of the Internet [reference 1].	**Move 1** **Step 1:** Claiming the centrality
The IoT concept, hence, aims at making the Internet even more immersive and pervasive. Furthermore, by enabling easy access and interaction with a wide variety of devices such as, for instance, home appliances, surveillance cameras, monitoring sensors, actuators, displays, vehicles, and so on, the IoT will foster the development of a number of applications that make use of the potentially enormous amount and variety of data generated by such objects to provide new services to citizens, companies, and public administrations.	**Move 1** **Step 2:** Making topic generalization
This paradigm indeed finds application in many different domains, such as home automation, industrial automation, medical aids, mobile healthcare, elderly assistance, intelligent energy management and smart grids, automotive, traffic management, and many others [reference 2].	**Move 1** **Step 3:** Reviewing items of previous research
However, such a heterogeneous field of application makes the identification of solutions capable of satisfying the requirements of all possible application scenarios a formidable challenge. This difficulty has led to the proliferation of different and, sometimes, incompatible proposals for the practical realization of IoT systems. Therefore, from a system perspective, the realization of an IoT network, together with the required backend network services and devices, still lacks an established best practice because of its novelty and complexity. In addition to the technical difficulties, the adoption of the IoT paradigm is also hindered by the lack of a clear and widely accepted business model that can attract investments to promote the deployment of these technologies [reference 3].	**Move 2** Establishing a niche

(Zanella, A., Bui, N., Castellani, A., Vangelista, L. & Zorzi, M. 2014. Internet of Things for smart cities. *IEEE Internet of Things Journal*, *1*(1): 22–32.)

The above excerpt is well written and quite typical in the first two moves. In the beginning, it arouses readers' interest by depicting a picture of our future with the Internet of Things (IoT).

This way of introducing the topic is effective not only in its vividness, but also in detailed elaboration on the characteristics of IoT. After the general introduction of the concept of IoT, the authors continue to provide more information, which points out the future application of IoT and its advantages. Then, a brief review of its application is made to pave the way for the current research. Move 2 is realized through a counter-claim that approves the wide application of IoT as well as states the challenge faced accordingly. The negation used to point out the problem the state-of-art IoT is mainly lexical, such as *challenge (n.), difficulty (n.), lack (v. & n.), hinder (v.), incompatible (adj.)*. This avoids direct negation such as the use of some negative quantifiers, which is a euphemistic presentation of the limitation of previous work. By doing so, the authors clarify their stance and also make their evaluation of the previous work more acceptable to the audience, especially those who have made contributions to the field.

2.3.5 Language Focus: Polarity and Modality

You might have noticed that when determining the research gap, the authors usually does not directly deny the previous works nor use assertive words to point out the limitation of them. "It is believed that the use of not in conjunction with many verbs is seen as providing a potentially hostile depiction of previous work" (Swale, 1990, p. 156). To weaken this hostility, they choose relatively mild lexical terms or expressions to show their academic rigor.

The mild argumentation is usually realized through Polarity and Modality. Polarity refers to the "opposition between positive ('It is.' 'Do that!') and negative ('It isn't.' 'Don't do that!')" (Halliday & Matthiessen, 2014, p. 172), so it is "a choice between yes and no", which, however, is not the only possibility; "there are intermediate degrees, various kinds of indeterminacy that fall in between, such as 'sometimes' or 'maybe'. [...] What the modality system does is to construe the region of uncertainty that lies between 'yes' and 'no'." (Halliday & Matthiessen, 2014, p. 176).

"In a proposition, the meaning of the positive and negative pole is asserting and denying" (Halliday & Matthiessen, 2014, p. 177). In between these two poles are those intermediate degrees, which are in two kinds: (1) degrees of probability, such as *certainly, probably, possibly*; (2) degrees of usuality, such as *always, usually, sometimes*. Both probability and usuality can be realized in three ways: (1) by a modal verb, such as *will, can, may*; (2) by a modal adjunct of probability or usuality, such as *probably, usually*; (3) by both together, such as *will probably, may possibly* (Halliday & Matthiessen, 2014, p. 177).

Probability and usuality can be used in a proposition to weaken the assertiveness, for example,

> * *It is foreseen that many...<u>will</u> provide...across millions of simple and <u>sometimes</u> tiny devices.*

* On the other hand, ...<u>can be</u> managed by several managers at the same time. Moreover, many...and...<u>will be too limited in terms of</u>..., ..., and...to be able to operate properly using the current systems.
* In this paper, due to the nature of..., we <u>shall</u> design...that...
* Given..., multiple...functions plausibly <u>could</u> have generated them.
* A...<u>might</u> predict...to better anticipate..., but then <u>may have difficulty in</u>...
* However, in many applications, such as...and..., their...<u>may be unknown</u> and time-varying.
* Building on these..., several novel key concepts have been proposed for next generation 5G networks, out of those, ...is <u>probably</u> the most important one.
* However, these studies assumed a...containing...in their experiments, whereas in actual situations, novel classes <u>always</u> appear.
* However, prior...and...are <u>often</u> unknown in practice, implying the estimation <u>may</u> require...
* This difficulty has led to...and <u>sometimes</u> incompatible proposals for the practical realization of...
* The...search has the property that it <u>will always</u>...
* ...is the general trend in the...research due to its..., which <u>often can</u> have several issues as discussed in...

2.4 Occupying the Niche

Once the research niche is established, we need to attempt to occupy it. "The role of Move 3 is to turn the niche established in Move 2 into the research space that justifies the present article" (Swales, 1990, p. 159). To be specific, Move 3 is the development of Move 2. It substantiates the counter-claim that has been made, fills the research gap created, answers the specific question raised or continues the tradition established in Move 2 (Swales, 1990, p. 159). In other words, the focus of Move 3 has shifted from previous work to the current research. Therefore, it is required to outline the purpose or state the nature of the present work.

2.4.1 The Purpose of the Current Research

After introducing the general research field and establishing the research space, the authors can finally set about introducing their own research. This process is from general to specific from Move 1 to Move 3. The focus flows from the general research field to some previous work and then to the current research. In this Move, the most essential part is to clearly tell the readers why you do this research, and what you want from it, and why it is important.

* The purpose of this paper is to give a complete description of the challenge, for two purposes: first to acquaint the reader with the state of the art in..., and secondly to provide guidance and lessons learnt for the benefit of...in future.
* This paper aims to solve both of these problems and thus address the two main drawbacks of...approaches...and lack of a...
* In addition, specific details of the...aspects of...are not well-documented in the literature; this paper aims to fill the gap.
* While the former problem has the optimal outcome, it is unclear as to...due to...in the latter. This paper provides an answer to this question.
* This paper addresses the need for...with...tools in evaluations of...protocols.
* This paper builds upon the...to demonstrate an approach leveraging...to address..., ..., and...for next generation...
* This paper explores in detail the use of...to image...within the network area.
* This paper proposes novel...and...methods using the...model.
* This paper intends to provide...and...concepts for...using...
* This paper is intended to provide an in-depth treatment of some of the aspects and techniques associated with...
* This paper introduces two new aspects to consider when...
* The main objective of this paper is to design a...strategy for...that is...
* The goal of this paper is to develop a data-driven approach to design...to... with unknown parameters, against...
* The goal of this work is to improve...to answer the following questions.
* The aim of the survey is to assess the state of the art in..., with an emphasis on...and...of...
* In this paper, we extend the results of [reference] in order to obtain a..., and to ensure...without increasing...

2.4.2 The Main Features of the Current Research

The authors can also state the main contribution, describe the important features/results, or briefly introduce the methodology of their research.

* In particular, this paper contributes to the design of a new...architecture for...using...technology.
* In essence, the main contributions of this paper are as follows: We formulate a...problem in the...Network with...constraints, and we show that...for this problem is hard.
* In this paper, we propose a...for...systems with...

* *In this paper, we present a new dataset and framework for the problem, and perform larger comparisons both in term of the methods and the metrics considered.*
* *In this paper, we show that there is nearly no capacity-delay tradeoff for...*
* *The main contributions of this paper are as follows...*
* *Our contributions can be summarized in the following steps: ...*
* *One of the novel contributions presented in this work is the...tool.*
* *In this paper, we improve over the previous approach in different ways.*
* *In this paper, we evaluate the most promising...in the literature, propose new algorithms and improvements to existing ones, present a method for performing...and..., and discuss the problem of...to very large data sets using ...*
* *Thus, in this paper, we cast all of our previous work in a...approach for..., and elucidate practices that will allow...to compare...and...results in a more unified manner.*
* *In this work, we consider...acquired using...and investigate a new...algorithm that does not rely on..., but on...*
* *We describe...adopted for the realization of...and report some of the...that have been collected by the system in its first operational days.*
* *Most previous attempts have proposed to stitch together existing solutions of the above sub-problems, in order to... In contrast, we would like to present in this work a...model that takes...as...and is trained to...*
* *Our main contribution in this work is a method able to... This work is an extension of the one presented in [reference]. In this paper, we improve over the previous approach in different ways. First, we allow... This brings more flexibility to the model which... Also, we introduce a new term in the minimization... Furthermore, we show how our method can be used when... Lastly, in this paper, we present a new dataset and framework for the problem, and perform larger comparisons both in terms of...and... Our results outperform the rest of the algorithms both quantitative and qualitatively.*
* *Unlike most research in this field and our previous work in [reference], in this paper a...scenario of...is considered.*

2.4.3 Language Focus

1) V-ing as a Result

When you establish your research niche by pointing out the limitations or research gap of previous research, you may need to elaborate on the result of the limitation or gap, so as to highlight the significance or contribution of your research. A *(thus)* + *v-ing* clause of result would be "particularly useful as alternatives to traditional logical connectors like *therefore* and *as a result*" (Swales & Feak, 2012, p. 115). For example:

Main clause	Ideally, this federated infrastructure will involve cloud resources at the mobile edge,
(Optional *thus/thereby*) + *v-ing*	thus bringing services as close to end users as possible.

More sentence patterns are shown below:

* We relate such a...to..., and show that in..., ...reduces..., <u>thus establishing</u> a connection to...principles.
* This objective can be pursued by the deployment of..., i.e., a...that provides...access to..., <u>thus unleashing</u> potential synergies <u>and increasing</u>...
* We evaluate the...properties of...as a whole, <u>thus showing</u> the benefits of combining the two modules.
* This is the most widely-used formulation, estimating...from..., <u>thereby using</u> a...without...
* Their biggest advantage, however, is the fact that they can be..., <u>thereby making</u>...
* The goal of the contest is to advance the development of...that can..., such as..., <u>resulting in</u>...
* Indeed, ...are processed sequentially, <u>resulting in</u> a...which is important for...
* As opposed to other solutions, the design operates in a single smart contract, <u>simplifying</u> the whole process in...<u>and reducing</u>...
* Although there is not yet a formal and widely accepted definition of..., the final aim is to..., <u>increasing</u> the quality of..., <u>while reducing</u> the operational costs of...
* For..., ...allows to..., <u>adjusting</u>...to the...needs.
* Using the...methods in [reference] might cause frequent and unnecessary..., <u>leading to</u>...
* This has naturally increased the confidence in..., <u>leading to</u> the idea of using...to support...
* Our...has some critical differences with these well-studied..., in terms of...and..., and hence, the results established for them do not directly apply in our case, <u>making</u> our theoretical results on the existence of..., interesting and nontrivial.
* In the past, these systems were stand alone and isolated from the world, <u>making</u> them unsusceptible to...

2) The Use of Deictic Signals

As mentioned before, the focus of Move 3 is on the current research. Therefore, in this move, the authors tend to use more deictic elements to refer to the present research, such as *this, the present, we, here, now, herein* (Swales, 1990, p. 159).

Chapter 2
Introducing Background

> * <u>Our work</u> in this area shows that...can introduce...to secure these systems.
> * Toward <u>this goal,</u> <u>we</u> propose a...that measures...
> * <u>In this paper,</u> <u>we</u> present a new architecture for...
> * <u>The objective of this paper</u> is to discuss...framework for the design of a(n)...
> * <u>The work presented in this paper</u> differs from our earlier results in the following three aspects.
> * Different to <u>the objectives of the present paper,</u> all of these methods, while referred to as..., require the knowledge of...for design and implementation.
> * <u>The following list</u> summarizes <u>the contributions of the present work</u>.
> * The other method is an earlier version of the current work, with a different algorithm that consistently underperforms the one we will introduce <u>here</u> as it is shown in the Results section.
> * The game introduced <u>herein</u> is a...game for which...solutions are sought.

3) This + Summary Noun

The pattern *This/These + summary noun* is a good way to establish connection with previous sentence. It avoids repetition as well as makes the sentence compact.

> * <u>We develop a...architecture utilizing...knowledge</u> to... <u>This approach</u> leverages...to provide...and...through...
> * ...<u>will increase</u> sevenfold between...(year) and...(year), reaching...per month by the end of...(year), and...will account for over x% of the total... <u>This trend</u> will cause a...due to...
> * ...<u>is extended</u> to include...and... <u>This development</u> improves performance and boosts the...properties of the algorithm, meaning that...is possible.
> * However, such a...application <u>makes</u>...capable of satisfying the requirements of...<u>a formidable challenge. This difficulty</u> has led to the...and, sometimes, ... for...
> * ..., ...and...are just few of the performance metrics that <u>5G networks</u> are expected to boost when deployed. <u>This game changer</u> relies on...such as...or...
> * While..., these...systems <u>are limited to</u>... <u>This limitation</u> can cause...when...and consequently affects...

▶ 2.5 Stating the Outline of the Article

In some journals, there is a Move about the overall structure of the article in the end of the Introduction. Here are some examples:

* *In this article, we first revisit..., originally cast in...framework, through... descriptions. Next, we show that this result can be used to get a... Concluding remarks are given in Section VII.*
* *This article is structured as follows. Section 2 reviews relevant works in the literature. Section 3 presents our vision and architecture for...in a...context. We then propose schemes for...(Section 4) and...(Section 5). In Section 6, we... The process of..., is described in Section 7...experiments on the performance of the overall...system follow in Section 8. We conclude the article in Section 9.*
* *The remainder/rest of this paper is organized as follows. Section 2 summarizes/reviews... Section 3 describes... Section 4 illustrates... Section 5 introduces... Section 6 presents... Finally, Section 7 concludes the paper.*
* *The remainder of this paper is organized as follows. The system model of...is described in Section II, including...and... Three conventional...methods are introduced in Section III, including... Following a discussion on the key issues when conducting the conventional...methods in..., the novel two-stage method is proposed in Section IV. An analysis of...for the proposed method is given in Section IV. Simulation results are presented in Section IV. Finally, conclusions are drawn in Section VII.*

In the corpus, some verbs that are often used in this part are: *address, consider, detail, design, discuss, describe, develop, evaluate, illustrate, present, propose, provide, show, utilize,* etc.

Chapter 2
Introducing Background

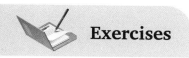 **Exercises**

I. Please identify the moves and specific steps in the following Introduction and comment on them.

Excerpt	Comment
Unlike the previous generation of mobile networks, 5G systems, are expected to rely on both the advancement of physical infrastructures represented by the introduction of Millimeter waves, massive MIMO, full duplex, beamforming, and small cells; as well as the emergence of SDN and NFV. By introducing the logical infrastructure abstraction, the 5G mobile networks will revamp modern network infrastructures using SDN and NFV as key enabling technologies towards softwarized networks. Network Softwarization is the core concept supporting the 5G's use cases, i.e., enhanced Mobile Broadband (eMBB), Ultra-Reliable and Low Latency Communications (uRLLC), and massive Machine Type Communication (mMTC), reducing both the Capital Expenditures (CAPEX) and the OPEX of the service provider, while keeping the deployment schema simple. Network Softwarization can enable high performance improvements by offering the flexibility and modularity that are required to create multiple overlying networks. These softwarized networks' mechanisms give place to a new concept dubbed Network Slicing. Meanwhile, the Third Generation Partnership Project (3GPP), in its Releases 15 and 16, introduced a service-oriented 5G core network (5GCN) that entirely relies on NFs, which increases the need for autonomous mechanisms to deploy and manage NS through operating multiple Service Function Chains (SFC) that will dynamically steer the network traffic and flows across multiple logical and physical infrastructures. For instance, a given user has a network slice that consists of two SFCs: The first one is used to handle the control plane part by steering the traffic through the Access and Mobility Management Function (AMF) and the Session Management Function (SMF) which are equivalent to the MME, PDN-Gateway Control plane (P-GWCP), and Serving-Gateway Control plane (S-GWCP) in the 4G system after the control and user plane separation of EPC nodes (CUPS). The second SFC will ensure the reliability of the data plane by steering the data flows from the AMF to the Data Network (DN) passing by the User plane Function (UPF) which represents the P-GW User plane (P-GWUP) and the S-GW User plane (S-GWUP) in the CUPS architecture.	

(Continued)
Excerpt	**Comment**
As the standards development organizations (SDOs), i.e., the Next Generation Mobile Network Alliance (NGMN), 3GPP, and International Telecommunication Union Telecommunication Standardization Sector (ITU-T), are instantiating network slices that contain one or more SFCs, each SFC composed by a set of NFs running inside either a logical node or a physical node. To enable this emerging approach, many NFs may require being traversed in a certain strict order, leveraging on the flexibility of NFV, Mobile Network Operators (MNOs) can deploy any particular slice type honoring its real-time requirements. However, this flexible management can lead to a huge number of active nodes in the network infrastructure that are scarcely used, which leads to an inefficient network slicing deployment. Based on these observations, the contributions of this paper are: ● The introduction of a new architecture in compliance with the ETSI-NFV model and the 3GPP specifications to create a fine-grained NS; ● The formulation of a Mixed Integer Linear Programming (MILP) to achieve an efficient cross-domain network slicing deployment regardless the underlying topologies (both the VNF layer and the physical layer) while satisfying all constraints and the specifications requested by the end-users or a given vertical's application; ● The design and evaluation of a heuristic algorithm to overcome the exponential runtime and allow a quick decision-making capability. The remainder of this paper is organized as follows. Section 2 summarizes the fundamental background topics and related research works. Section 3 describes the proposed architecture and our network model. Section 4 illustrates the problem formulation and describes our proposed framework solution. Section 5 introduces the proposed heuristic for the reduction of the exponential runtime. Section 6 presents the performance evaluation and our results analysis. Finally, Section 7 concludes the paper.	

(Addad, R. A., Bagaa, M., Taleb, T., Dutra, D. L. C. & Flinck, H. 2019. Optimization model for cross-domain network slices in 5G networks. *IEEE Transactions on Mobile Computing*, 19(5): 1156–1169.)

II. Please try to weaken the statements by adding probability and usuality.

1. Flexibility comes at a cost of robustness, especially when automated parameter estimation is involved.

Chapter 2
Introducing Background

2. It is a problem in various fields that one runs into a series of tasks that appear to be highly related to each other, yet applying the optimal machine learning solution of one problem to other results in poor performance.

3. In the context of secure control, attack detection and resilience schemes are divided in data driven and knowledge-based approaches.

4. We test the hypothesis that DL construct feature extractors that are more appropriate than selected adhoc features picked via automatic selection.

5. Answers to this question have a major practical impact especially in those situations where identifying a process model can be difficult and time consuming.

6. This difficulty has led to the proliferation of different and incompatible proposals for the practical realization of IoT systems.

7. However, acquiring these parameters is troublesome and costly.

8. Some of these agents are unreliable, and therefore the consensus process needs to be reliant.

9. An observed sequence of patterns conveys a meaning to the observer, whereby independent fragments of this sequence is hard to decipher in isolation.

10. Assuming robust deep learning is achieved, it is possible to train such a hierarchical network on a large set of observations and later extract signals from this network to a relatively simple classification engine for the purpose of robust pattern recognition.

III. Fill in each of the blanks with a summary noun to make the two sentences logically connected.

1. In statistics and data analysis, one typically proceeds from data presented in the form of real numbers or categorical values, implicitly assuming the underlying measurement process to be precise and exact. In many cases, however, this _____ is clearly not warranted.

2. We shall now introduce three categories of prediction problems, all of key relevance to the operations and management of commercial mobile wireless networks. This _____ is not meant to be exhaustive, although vast majority of problems we have encountered fall into one of these categories.

3. Many machine learning techniques are tied to a series of hyper-parameters and/or selection of sub-components that need to be tuned. This _____ can broadly be defined as the algorithm configuration problem.

4. In the context of formation control, most of the proposed approaches are based on the notion of navigation function, which is constructed from the geometric information on the considered topology and then employed to define gradient descent control laws. This _____ has been recently extended to the multi-agent scenario, both in a centralized and decentralized implementation.

5. Any successful attack on CPS may jeopardize critical infrastructure and people's lives and properties, even threaten national security. In 2010, Stuxnet malware launched a devastating attack on Iranian uranium enrichment facilities. This _____ raised a great deal of attention to CPS security in recent years.

6. Although there is not yet a formal and widely accepted definition of "Smart City", the final aim is to make a better use of the public resources, increasing the quality of the services offered to the citizens, while reducing the operational costs of the public administrations. This _____ can be pursued by the deployment of an urban IoT.

7. During the first three decades of research, the fuzzy logic community has more focused on topics in the realm of knowledge and information processing, such as control and approximate reasoning, and less on analyzing and learning from data. This _____ started to change in the recent past, which has been characterized by a shift from largely knowledge-based to strongly data-driven fuzzy modeling.

8. Comprehensibility was defined as the learning algorithm ability for encoding its model in such a way that it may be inspected and understood by humans. This _____ narrows the focus to the model itself.

9. Baseline PI is extended to include an appropriate combination of PI task selection and soft-max task selection. This _____ improves performance and boosts the exploratory properties of the algorithm, meaning that escape from local minima is possible.

10. We define a matrix-valued function, for each agent, which is similar in spirit to the definition of a standard navigation function. This _____ is modified by the presence of additional dynamics and the resulting value functions are smooth, hence yielding smooth control laws.

IV. Please combine the two sentences by a *v-ing* clause.

1. The application of the IoT paradigm to the Smart City is particularly attractive to local and regional administrations that may become the early adopters of such technologies. This application acts as catalyzers for the adoption of the IoT paradigm on a wider scale.

2. These two modules exploit different sets of relations and different model knowledge to perform detection. They compensate each other's vulnerabilities, and reduce the number of attacks that are stealthy.

3. Recent neuroscience findings have provided insight into the principles governing information representation in the mammalian brain. This leads to new ideas for designing systems that represent information.

4. In the past, these systems were standalone and isolated from the world. This makes them unsusceptible to external malicious attacks.

5. A blockchain contains a set of blocks, and every block contains a hash of the previous block. This creates a chain of blocks from the genesis block to the current block.

6. To the best of the authors' knowledge, this is the first time deep learning is introduced to the domain of psychophysiology. This yields efficient computational models of affect.

7. A simultaneous proliferation of high-value connected devices makes the IoT a desirable attack surface, and drives security-related resource requirements. This demands high-powered computation—lest a platform become unfavorable for mission-critical applications.

8. They successfully managed to learn decoding rules with high accuracy using only a fraction of the training trials required by the earlier approaches. This allows subjects to communicate consistently with a computer in a single session.

9. The study compares DL against ad-hoc feature extraction on physiological signals, used broadly in the AC literature. It shows that DL yields models of equal or significantly higher accuracy when a single signal is used as model input.

10. Batches of random experiences are drawn from the buffer and used for updates. This forces the network to generalize beyond what it is currently doing in the environment.

Chapter 3
Describing Methods

3.1 Lead-in

What make a good experimental procedure? Mark your answer with a √.

Have you included a description and size for all experimental and control groups?	
Have you included a step-by-step list of all procedures?	
Have you described how to change the independent variable and how to measure that change?	
Have you explained how to measure the resulting change in the dependent variable or variables?	
Have you explained how the controlled variables will be maintained at a constant value?	
Have you specified how many times you intend to repeat the experiment (should be at least three times), and is that number of repetitions sufficient to give you reliable data?	
Can another individual duplicate the experiment based on the experimental procedure you have written?	
If you are doing an engineering or programming project, have you completed several preliminary designs?	

(Retrieved from Science Buddies Organization website.)

The section of Methods deals with what we did or how we did it (Boxman & Boxman, 2020). It is an explicit bridge between literature review and the Results section. It describes the progression of procedure steps and provides sufficient details for replication studies (Cotos et al., 2017). To be specific, it describes in detail how the research is conducted, what experimental apparatus are needed, how to set up the apparatus, what the experimental procedures are, what materials are used, and how to develop the model or how to derive the model equations.

A descriptive model of methods is adopted in this book. Cotos et al.'s (2017) Demonstrating Rigour and Credibility model (for short DRaC) is adjusted to better describe the Methods section in IEEE journals. This model consists of three basic moves and several steps within each move:

- **Move 1: Contextualizing study methods**

    Step 1 Stating the purpose of the method

    Step 2 Referencing previous works

Step 3 Identifying the methodological approach

- **Move 2: Describing the study**

  Step 1 Rationalizing your method

  Step 2 Describing the data

  Step 3 Describing experimental/study procedures

- **Move 3: Establishing credibility**

3.2 Contextualizing Study Methods

You can begin your Methods section by providing necessary background information for the research method, setting the scene for experimental procedure details and explaining the procedures (Cotos et al., 2017).

3.2.1 Stating the Purpose of the Method

Instead of directly elaborating on how the research is conducted with the specific experiment, apparatus or methods, authors usually can briefly introduce the section by stating the "overview of the purpose of the method and the overall principle by which it works" (Boxman & Boxman, 2020, p. 34).

The following excerpt is the introductory part of the Methods section.

Excerpt	Comment
① In this section, we discuss the control design technique proposed to solve the multi-agent collision avoidance problem. ② Since Nash equilibria for the differential game introduced in Problem 2 cannot be easily obtained, a systematic method for constructing feedback control laws, which satisfy partial differential inequalities (PDIs) (instead of equations), leading to ea-Nash (instead of Nash) equilibria, is provided. ③ The method requires only the solution of matrix algebraic inequalities, which is provided in closed-form. ④ It is shown that the constructive design methodology, which leads to approximate solutions of the differential game in Problem 2, yields a solution to the original Problem 1.	Sentence ① is an overview of what the authors do in this section. Sentences ② and ③ explain in detail how the method works. Then, the last sentence briefly states the feasibility of the method used.

(Mylvaganam, T., Sassano, M. & Astolfi, A. 2017. A differential game approach to multi-agent collision avoidance. *IEEE Transactions on Automatic Control*, *62*(8): 4229–4235.)

There are some other patterns of writing an introductory part of a Methods section. Some are brief, for example:

Excerpt	Comment
III. Implementation ① We developed a proof of concept (PoC) implementation of the decentralized access control system in order to test and evaluate it. ② The following section provides additional details about our implementation, in particular regarding the IoT devices, management hub, and the blockchain network.	Sentence ① directly points out what system the authors developed in the methodology part and its purpose. Sentence ② provides an overview of the Methods section.

(Novo, O. 2018. Blockchain meets IoT: An architecture for scalable access management in IoT. *IEEE Internet of Things Journal*, 5(2): 1184–1195.)

Some syntactic patterns to begin a Methods section by stating the purpose are shown in the following:

* *In this section, we discuss how...can be used to get...algorithms.*
* *In this section we describe the proposed...model and discuss its characteristics.*
* *This section is an overview of our system with a...description. Later sections develop further details.*
* *This section provides information regarding the test material used, test settings, and logistics.*
* *In this section, we present our proposed scheme in details that comprise V1-ing, V2-ing, ...and Vn-ing.*
* *Our system follows the...approach: It first..., then..., and finally... The main steps are the following...*
* *This section describes...for solving..., and introduces a technique for...*
* *In this paper, we present a...method that takes... For simplicity we explain the method for the case of... Later on, we will show how to handle as well... The main steps of our method can be outlined as follows...*
* *In this section, we demonstrate how...techniques can be used to... We also show how...and...can be combined to achieve greater playing performance. Finally, we describe an attempt to...by means of..., which—albeit eventually failing—inspired us to investigate..., which will be reported in Section IV.*
* *In the present section we describe the evaluation design for our challenge tasks. Before this, we describe the requirements gathering process that we conducted, and the considerations that fed into our final designs.*
* *In this section we show how to directly estimate... Moreover, we show how this can be formulated as a...problem for which the...solution can be computed efficiently.*
* *This section provides the preliminary details about..., followed by the working of the proposed...framework for...in...*

> *   *This section is devoted to developing a...procedure to infer the system parameters, based on which, we show how to design...and prove that... Throughout the section, we make the following assumptions...*
> *   *In general, a conventional system for..., depicted in Figure x, consists of three main steps: x, y, and z, and it contains the following methods...*
> *   *In Section III-A, we present the underlying idea of...and provide an intuitive explanation why... Section III-B then includes a more rigorous mathematical description. In Section III-C, we discuss Z and in Section III-D the computational complexity.*
> *   *For...we introduce three conventional...methods: A, B, and C. The process of those methods is elaborated in this section, while their respective drawbacks when applied to a hybrid network are discussed in Section IV-A.*
> *   *The set of...protocols are referred to as..., which has the following tasks: (i) resolving...; (ii) performing...; (iii) decoding metadata and data; and (iv) interacting with... Its operation has to be designed according to the...requirements and to the...patterns of the supported services. In this section, we consider several...options for...services.*
> *   *The...problem is very dependent on...since it is a requirement for... The model used in this paper should take into account the...aspects of... Here, we present an augmented mathematical model of...for the development of a...system. Section IV-A develops a...model along with its...dynamics, and Section IV-B introduces a...model used for the development of...*

3.2.2 Referencing Previous Works

You can also situate some aspects of your method in the literature by means of citations, footnotes, and some relatively detailed descriptions of methods in important studies (Cotos et al., 2017). If the article is a review of a specific field, the Methods section can also begin by reviewing previous literature and/or indicating its development in future. For example:

Excerpt	Comment
① Artificial Immune Systems (AIS) emerged in the 1990s as a new branch in Computational Intelligence (CI). ② A number of AIS models exist, and they are used in pattern recognition, fault detection, computer security, and a variety of other applications researchers are exploring in the field of science and engineering [reference]. ③ Although the AIS research has been gaining its momentum, the changes in the fundamental methodologies have not been dramatic. ④ Among various mechanisms in the biological immune system that are explored as AISs, negative selection, immune network model and clonal selection are still the most discussed models [reference].	Sentence ① introduces the model by stating its origin. Sentence ② introduces its application. Then, Sentence ③ acknowledges the achievement of the method as well as states its status quo. Sentence ④ specifies the situation brought about in the previous sentence by presenting the most discussed models.

(Dasgupta, D. 2006. Advances in artificial immune systems. *IEEE Computational Intelligence Magazine*, *1*(4): 40–49.)

For an original research article, the reference of related previous works is to facilitate the understanding of the current method.

Excerpt	Comment
① In this work we built on the multi-scale fusion principles to propose a single image underwater dehazing solution. ② Image fusion has shown utility in several applications such as image compositing, multispectral video enhancement, defogging, and HDR imaging. ③ Here, we aim for a simple and fast approach that is able to increase the scene visibility in a wide range of underwater videos and images. ④ Similar to [23] and [54], our framework builds on a set of inputs and weight maps derived from a single original image. ⑤ In contrast to [23] and [54] however, those ones are specifically chosen in order to take the best out of the white-balancing method introduced in the previous section. ⑥ In particular, as depicted in Fig.1, a pair of inputs is introduced to respectively enhance the color contrast and the edge sharpness of the white-balanced image, and the weight maps are defined to preserve the qualities and reject the defaults of those inputs, i.e., to overcome the artifacts induced by the light propagation limitation in underwater medium. ⑦ This multi-scale fusion significantly differs from our previous fusion-based underwater dehazing approach published at IEEE CVPR. ⑧ To derive the inputs from the original image, our initial CVPR algorithm did assume that the backscattering component (due to the artificial light that hits the water particles and is then reflected back to the camera) has a reduced influence. ⑨ This assumption is generally valid for underwater scenes decently illuminated by natural light, but fails in more challenging illumination scenarios, as revealed by Fig. 11 in the results section. ⑩ In contrast, this paper does not rely on the optical model and proposes an alternative definition of inputs and weights to deal with severely degraded scenes. ⑪ As depicted in Fig. 8 and detailed below, our underwater dehazing technique consists in three main steps: inputs derivation from the white balanced underwater image, weight maps definition, and multi-scale fusion of the inputs and weight maps.	Sentence ① presents the overview of the purpose of the method as well as the overall principles by which it works. Sentences ② and ③ explain the application of this method and its advantages and purpose. Sentences ④ and ⑤ compare and contrast the current approach with and to the previous ones, and propose the framework of the current research. Sentence ⑥ states the overview of the method with a figure. Sentence ⑦ points out the novelty the current method has compared with the authors' previous method. Sentences ⑧ and ⑨ then describe the assumption of their previous methods, and also evaluate its positive and negative sides. Accordingly, Sentence ⑩ proposes the current method that can remedy the previous ones. Sentence ⑪ briefly introduces the steps that the current method takes.

(Ancuti, C. O., Ancuti, C., De Vleeschouwer, C. & Bekaert, P. 2018. Color balance and fusion for underwater image enhancement. *IEEE Transactions on Image Processing*, 27(1): 379–393.)

Chapter 3
Describing Methods

Some syntactic patterns to build the current method in the context of the accepted methods in the field are shown in the following:

* *In [reference], we have presented... Even though...has proven its capability in..., there are cases that... // ...is a real-world challenge that is quite common in... In [reference] and [reference], we have investigated...using...and...models for... However, in this paper, we have improved our...by adding the following elements.*
* *In this paper, ...is computed by employing...method we have introduced in [reference], which stems from the concept of... The main concept of...is...in order to obtain an improved...*
* *Our...scheme is an extension of...methods that has a larger flexibility [reference]. It also partitions a frame into...which... However, in contrast to..., binary splits into blocks of unequal size are supported. More precisely, ...*
* *Different...systems have been proposed in the past to...[reference]. Nowadays, most of the...are...systems, in which...*
* *...represent...characterized by...In [reference], ...was defined as...In this work, we extend the...by adding explicit process descriptors.*
* *In this section, we propose a...that enables... While...is traditionally formulated as..., it would be based on...and therefore lack... In contrast, we propose to represent...using...that characterize... We will show that such a...is essential to guaranteeing some desirable properties for saliency detection and shape matching.*
* *In this section, the...model will be obtained with the use of a...strategy. In particular, a...will be used since such a strategy has been shown to provide better...properties of the system than its relative degree one equivalent.*
* *The developed...incorporates all the benefits from state-of-the-art...techniques of both the...and... Before we outline the architecture and behavior of..., we briefly introduce the mentioned...and motivate our selection of adequate candidate tools.*
* *To conduct our experiments, it was necessary to prepare a large-scale...dataset that contains... The...dataset has been used in...contexts. However, ... Therefore, this database does not fit our...problem setting, wherein... In this study, we built a...dataset collected by running a...application called...for about two years.*
* *Due to the identified trends in...regarding...and hence..., ...will be identified and analyzed in this section, coming from both industry as well as research environments.*
* *...is a...algorithm designed to handle large-scale datasets. // ...learns a set of rules following the...paradigm first used in...in the...system. This...paradigm generates...in which..., using a...to... Hence, ...is a rule. Once a rule is learnt, it is added to the rule set and the training set is filtered by removing all the examples covered by this rule. The...process generally stops when the whole training set is covered. However, the*

> *stopping criteria changes when using a default rule as detailed in Section 3.1. In the rest of the section, we only describe the aspects about...that are relevant to this work. For a full description of the algorithm, please see...*

3.2.3 Identifying the Methodological Approach

You can also specify "the approach or research design with brevity or elaboration", and "describe the setting" (Cotos et al., 2017, p. 97). For example, you explain the preparation for the experiment, experimental procedures or the setting up of the apparatus, or introduce the research subjects or participants.

Excerpt	Comment
① An experiment is designed to study mobile users' behavior and to develop a statistical model for the orientation of mobile devices that act as the receiver for wireless communication systems. ② During the experiment, 40 participants were asked to use their cellphones normally that create 222 datasets for orientation. ③ They were asked to use the cellphone in both portrait and landscape modes for one minute. ④ The orientation data is measured for both sitting and mobile users. ⑤ In the experimental measurement, the application Physics Toolbox Sensor Suite has been used as it can provide instantaneous rotation angles α, β and γ. ⑥ This application can be running in the background while the participants can perform activities that require data connection, e.g., browsing or watching streaming videos. ⑦ Below is a summary of the experimental setup: ● Activities while sitting: 1) Browsing twice in portrait mode, 2) Watching streaming videos twice in landscape mode, ● Activities while walking following a certain path: 1) Browsing in portrait mode, 2) Watching streaming videos in landscape mode. The path that the participants took was a straight corridor with dimensions of 40 m × 1.5 m. The participants were asked to walk down the corridor once. We note that the shape of the test area should not affect the experimental results and the model for the elevation angle as it mostly depends on the posture and physical attributes of typical users rather than the environment. This has been confirmed with sets of uncontrolled data collections from participants using their device in different environments.	Sentence ① states the purpose of the experiment. Sentences ② and ③ introduce how the experiment was conducted by a certain number of participants. Sentences ④ and ⑤ explain how the data is measured. Sentence ⑥ provides some supplementary information about the measurement of data. Sentence ⑦ sends a signal of the summary of the experimental setup. The rest of the paragraph provides some supplementary information about the participants.

(Soltani, M. D., Purwita, A. A., Zeng, Z., Haas, H. & Safari, M. 2018. Modeling the random orientation of mobile devices: Measurement, analysis and LiFi use case. *IEEE Transactions on Communications*, 67(3): 2157–2172.)

Some similar structures can also be used:

> * In this paper we apply different selection criteria to identify...that will be used by... The use of...allows us to apply the selection algorithm directly over...in the...domain, hence... // ...can be performed according to different parameters, such as... Our main focus is on...based on..., since our analysis is mostly based on...
> * To take...into account, it is necessary to... [characteristics of part of the method]. Hence, the proposed method determines..., which falls into three categories: A, B and C. Users in the first two categories are only granted access to a certain network. These users are handed over within the same network when needed. The third category allows...to... [conditions for the third category]. Based on the above categories, a...problem is formulated in this section. To..., a novel algorithm based on...is also proposed.
> * We describe a...method that...and yields... The framework for extracting this information is presented, along with a multiresolution approach. We assume..., and...are known or extracted from a previous characterization step. The...is used to obtain...information for... Here, we describe... Our method assumes that..., and we explore this assumption in Section III-C. By exploiting this information as prior knowledge, ...is achieved.

3.3 Describing the Study

This move is the main part of the methodology and is usually obligatory for any discipline. You need to describe "all the specifics of the study, focusing on what was done in the experimental procedure prior to data analysis and clarifying conditions, treatments, controls, data, tools, in-process judgements, etc." (Cotos et al., 2017, p. 97). You can arrange this part according to some logical order, for example, in the order in which the experiment is conducted or the different parameters considered in the method.

Based on the different specific procedures of the method, this part can be divided into different sub-sections, and you need to give each one a title to keep your readers aware of where they are. You should try to "use informative subheadings to help organize and present" your material and method by topic (Pechenik, 2016, p. 156). Here, "informative" means that you should be specific to provide enough information for your readers to understand the subsection. For example:

Informative	Uninformative
A. State Feedback Design and Data-Based Parametrization of All Stabilizing Controllers	A. Design and Parameters
B. Linear Quadratic Regulation	B. Experiment

3.3.1 Rationalizing Your Method

Before getting in touch with how your research is conducted, you can explain why the particular method is adopted with the following sentence structures.

* *The chosen...technology for our...was... We developed... We chose...since...*
* *Since...were used for..., we generated...models for..., as well as for...*
* *Since...is critical in..., we first apply our...technique to... This step aims at v-ing...by v-ing... [description of the function of this step]. As a result, to obtain our first input we perform...*
* *In order to..., ...must be estimated. To further..., ...can also be estimated.*
* *In order to analyse...and compare its performance with...we use...*
* *Our motivation was to...to... Our focus was on..., since... We also wished to... We decided to...*
* *Given the results stated in..., in order to design a...architecture, it is necessary either to..., or... To address the latter, ...could be added, although this may not be possible depending on the application.*
* *In the... problem, ...is given. The goal is to... In more formal terms, the goal is to find a Hamiltonian tour of minimal length on a fully connected graph.*
* *The X method has been widely used for solving...problems. Before comparing our proposed methods with the X method, this section summarizes the X method.*
* *In this section, based on the different characteristics between...and...in terms of..., we propose a...method for... The main contribution of this section is three-fold: i) analyse the key issues when...; ii) formulate the...process as a two-stage problem, which firstly determines...and then performs...; and iii) apply...to the first stage to... Regarding the second stage, a...method, such as the...and..., is applicable.*

3.3.2 Describing the Data

You can inform your readers about "the process of collecting, sampling, or selecting primary or secondary data", and present "the characteristics of the data" (Cotos et al., 2017, p. 98). The sentence structures can be used are as the following.

* *We denote a...as...with...*
* *We consider that..., denoted as..., that is atomic and cannot be divided into subtasks. Each... is characterized by a tuple of two parameters,..., in which... specifies..., and...specifies...*

Chapter 3
Describing Methods

> * *In our case, we consider only the per-sample energy cost of acquiring sensor data from...and...*
> * *The system to be controlled is open-loop unstable. The...procedure is implemented in MATLAB. We generate the data with...and by using...*
> * *In this paper, we developed a real-world testbed that... We have conducted...to gather realistic datasets containing...*
> * *In Section..., the measured data are...and..., and the starting point is to express the...and...in terms of the...data. Here, we show how similar arguments can be used when only input/output data are accessible.*
> * *For our experiments, we consider a...environment in the form of...*
> * *In a...method, ...denoted by..., selects all the...pixels found at...pixels from the current pixel. More exactly, ...is of size...and it is used as the...for the...model of the...method.*
> * *To conduct our experiments, it was necessary to prepare a large-scale...dataset that contains...and...The...dataset [reference] has been used in...contexts [reference]. However,... Therefore, this database does not fit our personalization problem setting, wherein...*

3.3.3 Describing Experimental/Study Procedures

You can illustrate how the experiment is completed step by step, and provide detailed description of the actions and their sequence (Cotos et al., 2017). For example,

Excerpt	Comment
A. Proxy Model ① The first step in developing a proxy is to select a system model. ② The accuracy and inputs to this model determine the performance of the data proxy. ③ For illustration purposes, we apply the vehicle motion model from Kumar et al. (2013). ④ The car is modeled as a unicycle with the constraint that it moves along a trajectory with no slip. ⑤ A Kalman filter is applied to estimate the location and the distance traveled by the vehicle (called system states here). ⑥ These estimates are performed at a baseline frequency while the model allows GpS and OBD speed measurements to be incorporated at varying frequencies in the estimation model. ⑦ Additionally, a scaling and bias correction are applied to accelerometer measurements for improved estimation accuracy. ⑧ To collect data, a vehicle was driven in a loop while recording information at the reference 10 Hz from a GpS device, an accelerometer, and an OBD interface. ⑨ We identified an optimal reference trajectory using fully sampled data run through our tuned Kalman filter. ⑩ We then iterated filtering using differing down sampling rates for OBD and GpS and calculated the costs and QoDs for each run, as described in the following sections.	This sub-section begins with an introduction of the specific step in Sentence ① and the characteristics of the model in Sentence ②. Sentence ③ explains the model this research adopts, followed by Sentence ④ to Sentence ⑧, which specify the procedures of the operation of this model. Sentences ⑨ and ⑩ then briefly describe how the authors processed the data obtained, connecting the following section.

(Siegel, J. E., Kumar, S. & Sarma, S. E. 2017. The future Internet of Things: Secure, efficient, and model-based. *IEEE Internet of Things Journal*. 5(4): 2386–2398.)

You can also use the following sentence structures.

* *This section describes…models that we used for… For the…problem, the following assumptions are made.*
* *A…channel is considered, where at the beginning of each time slot, a…is generated and stays fixed throughout that time slot.*
* *Following the law of iterated expectations, for target dimensions…, we obtain the predictive mean…with…*
* *In the following, the computation of…is considered. For simplicity, only…is considered for…, and the result is later generalized to…*
* *In the experiments reported later, we use…*
* *The experiments were done on…desktop with Intel… We used…and…, which is derived from…*
* *In this section, a procedure to systematically construct a set of dynamic strategies solving the…instead of the…is presented. The method, introduced in…, relies on the notion of…solution and a dynamic extension…, which is common to all agents.*
* *We define a…as…function that is guaranteed to…by… In this and the following subsections, we will analyze the properties of…module of… Note that, given that…, we consider…at… Hence, let us define…for clarity of exposition.*
* *First, we discuss the effect of the…parameter…upon the proposed… Second, we study the effect of the…factor…upon the proposed… Third, we discuss the effect of the…upon the proposed…*
* *In this subsection, we will present the complete algorithm in a…form. After that, the…scheme will be introduced in detail.*
* *We model the…problem as a game between… Let…denote…, each corresponding to a… The…is discretized into a finite set of… The information collection environment is then represented as…, where… The time is also assumed to be discretized into time steps. Next, we extend the model to incorporate…*
* *In the proposed approach, a…routine is integrated into the…algorithm and an X is constructed around the main program. Within the X different values of…are trialed until the best solution is obtained.*
* *In experiment set A, …were used to create different…and…tasks were trialed with… In experiment set B, …were used and…tasks were trialed with…values of… Each problem was solved using…, the…algorithm, and…extension.*
* *The…tests were carried out for four categories of…: A, B, C and D. The details of the test sequences are provided in Tables X and Y. The sequences are selected from different sources and have different…characteristics, which leads to different behavior of…algorithms. This is the first formal test of…standards where a wide range of…has been evaluated.*

Chapter 3
Describing Methods

3.4 Establishing Credibility

In this move, you can deliver information about the quality of analysis and imply that the study procedure results in valid and credible findings. You can do this with the following sentence structures.

* *We will show that the combined use of the two modules in...has advantages in terms of...*
* *In both scenarios, the...network grants all the requests to all the resources. In addition, the tests in both scenarios were performed with a different number of... Every test was measured...times, for...each time, to calculate the average values and the number of...ranged from...to... Furthermore, the second scenario achieves a steady throughput at...requests per...during all the tests. In this scenario, all the...request the resource information from a single...device and, as a result, the...limits the whole performance of this scenario.*
* *In the previous sections, we have considered...formulations based on... Besides their simplicity, one of the main reasons for resorting to such formulations is that... In this section, we exemplify this point by considering..., as well as the problem of..., which are both situations where...can be challenging.*
* *It has been proven that the proposed...scheme using the...model of...drives...to a specified vicinity of... This is an important property, since the ability to...illustrates... with respect to...*
* *It has been demonstrated that the proposed...scheme limits the error of...in the...mode. Furthermore, since..., ...implies that the new strategy ensures... The advantage of the new approach will be further highlighted in...in the next section.*
* *The proposed algorithm and...streams have been designed to enable... The algorithm in Fig. x can be parallelized as follows. First, ... Next, ... Most importantly, ... In addition, due to..., the results can be... We have implemented this using...for...architectures.*
* *We subsequently show that...is powerful enough to provide...that significantly outperforms several state-of-the-art...models. Since the existing features are robust enough, we focus our work on...that exploits the capabilities of these features for effective...*
* *To determine if..., [reference] assume that... Unfortunately, such approach is not very accurate. Additionally, ...also depends on... We therefore suggest a better measure by...As long as..., ...in (algorithm) holds. If..., on the other hand, the...no longer holds and...might be necessary, or...must be performed in...domain, see Section x.*

* We have already proven that... Therefore, we conclude that (algorithm A) implies (algorithm B). In order to obtain..., one may wish to... Therefore, it is reasonable to establish conditions ensuring that... For that purpose, in the last theorem, we determine the...ensuring that... We can notice from (algorithm C) that this implies...
* In this paper, the...parameter and the...factor are selected to lie within the ranges...and...respectively based on the above discussions. The...parameter ranges are specific to...presented in this paper, and perhaps other parameter ranges are more appropriate in other situations. Fortunately, our experience has indicated that...with the suggested parameter ranges exhibit good estimation performance in many contexts.
* The drawback of the...approach is that... As discussed above, ... This is especially critical for...as it may...

3.5 Figure Description

Methodology is usually accompanied with figure illustration, which constitutes an important part in the Methods section.

Figure description can be carried out with three steps:

(1) Overview of the purpose of the model/experiment/apparatus...and the overall principle by which it works (typically 1–2 sentences); and

(2) Description of the principal parts according to some logical order, i.e., spatial arrangement (e.g., top to bottom, left to right, center to outside) or functional arrangement (e.g., in the order in which the parts operate or process material or information, from the beginning to the end); and

(3) Functional description, detailing how the parts work together, preferably in the order in which the parts operate (Boxman & Boxman, 2020, p. 34).

3.5.1 Overview of the Purpose of the Model/Experiment/Apparatus and the Overall Principle by Which It Works

With a few sentences, you can briefly summarize the information shown in the figure. In this step, you need to explicitly point out which figure you are describing to guide your readers. For example, *Figure 1 is...*

You can use sentences with active voice like *Fig. x + reporting verb + noun phrase / that clause*. Here are some examples:

Chapter 3
Describing Methods

> * *Fig. x shows the results of the two scenarios.*
> * *Fig. x displays/reveals that...*
> * *Fig. x shows that for different..., ...remains valid.*
> * *Fig. x demonstrates the procedure for v-ing + object...*
> * *Fig. x illustrates a scheme that aims to...*
> * *Fix. x indicates a...diagram of the proposed scheme.*
> * *Fig. x presents a simplified view of...frameworks and shows how...*
> * *Fig. x presents a...system, which is comprised of three steps:...*
> * *Fig. x depicts the architecture overview suggested in this paper. We have divided the architecture into three layers, as it... The...layer consists of... In this layer, [description of the function of this layer]. The...layer consists of a set of... [description of the function of this layer]. The...layer consists of a set of..., e.g... [description of the function of this layer]. It is noticed that... For instance, ... In the following work, ...is considered, while...was not studied. However, the proposed solution can be also used to...if...*

You can also use sentences with passive voice like *The...is shown in Fig. x*. Notice that in English the passive forms are just as appropriate as the active forms (Swales & Feak, 2012).

> * *The...are represented in Fig. x.*
> * *The...diagram of...is shown in Fig. x.*
> * *The results for...are depicted in Fig. x.*
> * *This...technique is illustrated in Fig. x.*
> * *A visualization of the...is given in Fig. x.*
> * *An overview of the proposed...schemes for...can be seen in Fig. x.*
> * *An overview of...and...methodologies is illustrated in Fig. x.*
> * *An overview of the...methodologies is illustrated in Fig. x. There are four stages involved in the proposed method, namely, A, B, C and D. In A stage, there are two types of...data, that is, train and test...data. During the...phase... Subsequently, ... Finally, ...*
> * *The proposed model is depicted in Fig. x, in which...are assumed to be...*
> * *A...model at...GHz for the...environment using...with...is displayed in Fig. x.*
> * *The...of the proposed...is given in Fig. 1, and the functional details of each of the...are described as follows.*
> * *Illustrated in Fig. x is the...*
> * *We assume a...described in Fig. x.*
> * *We build the main blocks of our...on the...introduced in [reference] and illustrated in*

Fig. x.

* *We refer to this as a...method, and it is demonstrated in Fig. x.*
* *It is believed that a...in [reference] and shown in Fig. x may achieve...*
* *In Fig. 4, the top five important features in our dataset along with...are shown.*

You can also locate the figure with an *as clause* or a *prepositional phrase*. For example:

* *As shown in Fig. x, a...is selected for...depending on...*
* *As shown in Fig. x, we first extract...and then...*
* *As depicted in Fig. x, ...is introduced to...*
* *As illustrated in Fig. x, we start with...*
* *This module consists of two phases: ...and...as depicted in Fig. x.*
* *We propose a...to...as depicted in Fig. x.*
* *We consider a...system as illustrated in Fig. x, in which...is equipped with...to provide...*
* *According to Fig. x, in order to..., ...is first divided into...*
* *In Fig. x, we assume/illustrate that...*
* *In Fig. x, we illustrate three typical cases that can...*
* *We propose the...scheme of...whose...diagram is shown in Fig. x.*

3.5.2 Description of the Principal Parts of the Figure According to Some Logical Order

You need to explain, in a few sentences, the organization or main parts of your figure to help your readers understand it. The following sentense structures could be helpful:

* *The...of a...module can be seen in Fig. x. While this...is rated for..., it utilizes... Each...is composed of a...and a...operating at..., connected to... The...is operated using... There is a...with a... The...and...are independently controlled by respective...*
* *The...can be seen in Fig. x. The...is designed for...utilizing a... The X is comprised of a...connected to a..., followed by a...with...structure at the primary side, and a...on the secondary side. The X also has an additional... from a...that...*
* *To illustrate the main concepts of this section, we assume a...as pictured in Fig. 6. A...is equipped with a...that consists of a very large number of...while the...are equipped with one or possible small number of...*
* *Additionally, Fig. x shows that... As can be seen in the first...columns of Fig. x, using the...based on..., ...yields poor estimates. In contrast, by simply applying...on...we obtain comparable and even better estimates than the...techniques of...*

Chapter 3
Describing Methods

* As depicted in Fig. x and detailed below, our...technique consists in three main steps: A, B, and C. A. Since..., we first apply our...technique to... This step aims at... In..., ...suffers from...since... As a result, to obtain our first input we perform a... // ...aims at...and is relevant since...tend to... B. ...are used during...in such a way that... They are thus defined based on... C. ...

* As can be seen in Fig. x, the...modules integrated with...and...were able to... At each time step, ...would then...and... Upon completion of...timestep, ...would... This allows...to react to...by..., by..., and by... according to... After..., ...would then... until..., allowing...to..., i.e., ...

* Fig. x shows a small sample of... To guarantee..., each timestep is signaled by... Using..., ...is able to..., to be represented by... In the example shown...are instantiated at... Similarly...is able to...

* Fig. x shows... As can be seen..., which are represented as..., are exactly the same as provided by... The...also shows...

* Fig. x presents the...system, which is comprised of three steps: A, B and C. In general, based on..., the...system outputs..., which indicates... Here four parameters are considered as input: a, b, c, and d. Taking...deployment in Fig. y as an example, the...adjacent to...are... The...reflects...A...means... Consequently, this...will...if... The activity of...is defined as...

* Fig. x features the comparison between...and... In Fig. x, the left Y-axis represents the number of..., the right Y-axis shows..., and the X-axis shows the number of...in the proposed architecture. For the optimal solution, the number of...represented by the pentagon shape increases linearly from...to...when the number of...increases. It is noticed that the number of...follows a...logic which means that... The mean number of...is...with a standard deviation of... Meanwhile, the...showed as a hexagonal shape increases exponentially when... The...shows that the number of..., represented by the circle shape, increases from...to...when...is reached. The mean number of...is...with a standard deviation of... Concurrently, the..., portrayed by the star shape, increases linearly from...to... The linear regression parameters are...and..., as a and b, respectively, for the solution cost of our set of experiments.

3.5.3 Functional Description

Figure description often consists of two parts: caption and textual description. In the caption, you can briefly describe the main information delivered by the figure, while in the textual description, you need to specifically explain the functions of the figure.

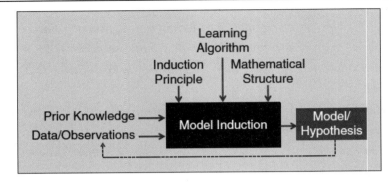

Fig. 3. Schematic presentation of the induction process (with possible feedback cycles) and its "ingredients": Model induction is realized by a learning algorithm that implements an induction principle and operates on the set of properly preprocessed data. Additional background knowledge is incorporated in various ways.

Excerpt	Comment
① As shown in Fig. 3, a typical model induction process requires several "ingredients".	Sentence ① is the overview of Fig. 3.
② In addition to the (training) data D itself, some sort of prior knowledge K is always needed—without any prior knowledge, data is meaningless and learning impossible. ③ In particular, such knowledge is needed to specify a suitable *hypothesis space* H, i.e., a restricted class of candidate models (hypotheses) h. ④ The task of a learning algorithm A essentially consists of choosing a candidate $h \in H$ that appears most promising in light of the data D. ⑤ Mathematically, a learning algorithm, or learner for short, can thus be thought of as a mapping $D \rightarrow H$, where D is the sample space (the set of all data sets D the learner may encounter as input of the induction process). ⑥ This mapping is based on an underlying induction principle, such as maximum likelihood estimation or empirical risk minimization.	The main part of the figure description illustrates how this model works. The description starts from the input of the model at the left of the figure (Sentence ②), and then emphasizes the importance of the prior knowledge for model hypothesis at the right (Sentence ③), followed by explanation of how the learning algorithm works at the top of the figure (Sentences ④, ⑤ and ⑥).

(Couso, I., Borgelt, C., Hullermeier, E. & Kruse, R. 2019. Fuzzy sets in data analysis: From statistical foundations to machine learning. *IEEE Computational Intelligence Magazine, 14*(1): 31–44.)

Chapter 3
Describing Methods

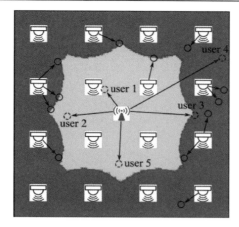

Fig. 3. Representative users for APS in a hybrid Li-Fi and Wi-Fi network.

Excerpt	Comment
① Fig. 3 demonstrates some representative users. Due to the presence of ICI in the Li-Fi network, cell-centre users (e.g., user 1) obtain a much higher SINR and thus a much higher spectrum efficiency than cell-edge users (e.g., user 2). Note that both user 1 and 2 would be connected to Wi-Fi if the SSS is applied. To reach the same data rate, user 2 requires more resource than user 1 if they are both switched to Li-Fi. Hence assigning user 2 to Wi-Fi is better than assigning user 1, though user 1 receives a stronger Wi-Fi signal than user 2 does. User 3 is in a situation similar to user 2, but locates in the field where the Wi-Fi SNR is lower than the Li-Fi SNR. In other words, user 3 is connected to Li-Fi when using the SSS method. Because of receiving a lower Wi-Fi SNR, user 3 has a lower priority than user 2 to use the Wi-Fi resource. However, not all of the Li-Fi cell-edge users should be switched to Wi-Fi. When a user experiences a very weak Wi-Fi signal (e.g., user 4), it would consume a substantial quantity of Wi-Fi resource. Therefore, this user is better to stay in the Li-Fi network in order to avoid draining the Wi-Fi resource. Another case is when the Li-Fi APs adjacent to a user are not in service (e.g., user 5). In this case, the user receives slight interference from distant Li-Fi APs, and thus is better to be served by Li-Fi so as to offload traffic from Wi-Fi.	Sentence ① summarizes the main information this figure provides. The rest of the figure description is developed in sequential order of how each user is connected to Wi-Fi or Li-Fi under different conditions.

(Wu, X., Safari, M. & Haas, H. 2017. Access point selection for hybrid Li-Fi and Wi-Fi networks. *IEEE Transactions on Communications*, *65*(12): 5375–5385.)

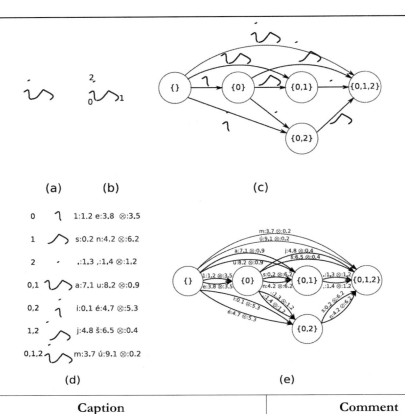

Caption	Comment
Fig. 3. Lattice creation: On the input ink (a), we determine cut points and create three segments (b). From the segments, we create a segmentation lattice (c) by grouping adjacent segments in character hypotheses. The character hypotheses are classified (d) and the lattice is labeled (e).	Overview of the figure and the main steps of lattice creation from (a) to the (e).

Excerpt	Comment
① Starting from the segmentation lattice (Fig. 3c), we create a multi-graph by adding edges for each potential label for each character hypothesis (Fig. 3e). ② These edges are assigned the classification result for the character hypotheses (Fig. 3d) as a label and the score for that label from the classifier as a cost which is later linearly combined with the other feature functions. ③ The garbage class is treated specially: Each edge is assigned an additional garbage feature function with a value corresponding to the classifier score for the garbage class.	The main part of the figure explains how to operate the lattice step by step, from segmentation to adding edges and then to assigning the edges classification result.

Chapter 3
Describing Methods

	(Continued)
④ For each character hypothesis we consider the top 20 classification results, thus the labeled lattice will have 20 times the edges as the segmentation lattice and the same set of nodes.	Sentence ④ explains how to get the lattice for each character.

(Keysers, D., Deselaers, T., Rowley, H. A., Wang, L. L. & Carbune, V. 2016. Multi-language online handwriting recognition. *IEEE Transactions on Pattern Analysis and Machine Intelligence*, *39*(6): 1180–1194.)

3.6 Language Focus

Passive voice is found being frequently used to describe a process in the Methods section. The focus of process description is usually not on the agent (the person who performs the action), but instead, it is on "explaining how something is done" (Swales & Feak, 2012, p. 120).

Excerpt	Comment
① An experiment is designed to study mobile users' behavior and to develop a statistical model for the orientation of mobile devices that act as the receiver for wireless communication systems. ② During the experiment, 40 participants were asked to use their cellphones normally that create 222 datasets for orientation. ③ They were asked to use the cellphone in both portrait and landscape modes for one minute. ④ The orientation data is measured for both sitting and mobile users. ⑤ In the experimental measurement, the application Physics Toolbox Sensor Suite has been used as it can provide instantaneous rotation angles, α, β and γ. ⑥ This application can be run in the background while the participants can perform activities that ALG distribution.	This description of an experiment consists of six sentences, each of which is about one step in the experimental procedure and is in passive voice. The focus of each sentence is on how the step is carried out, rather than who carries out the experiment.

Excerpt	Comment
① We design an experiment to study mobile users' behavior and to develop a statistical model for the orientation of mobile devices that act as the receiver for wireless communication systems. ② During the experiment, we asked 40 participants to use their cellphones normally that create 222 datasets for orientation. ③ We asked them to use the cellphone in both portrait and landscape modes for one minute. ④ We measure the orientation data for both sitting and mobile users. ⑤ In the experimental measurement, we have used the application Physics Toolbox Sensor Suite as it can provide instantaneous rotation angles, α, β and γ. ⑥ We can run this application in the background while the participants can perform activities that ALG distribution.	Compare this description with the above one. In this active voice version of experimental description, the repetition of the agent "we" does not provide any new information to the readers, because the readers are aware of who carries out the experiment, no matter whether he/she is made explicit in the text or not.

(Soltani, M. D., Purwita, A. A., Zeng, Z., Haas, H. & Safari, M. 2018. Modeling the random orientation of mobile devices: Measurement, analysis and LiFi use case. *IEEE Transactions on Communications*, 67(3): 2157–2172.)

While reading literature, you may find that not all the process description is made of passive voice sentences. Sometimes, both active voice and passive voice are used.

Excerpt	Comment
① First, the handover cost caused by light-path blockages is considered. ② Users in the category "WiFi only" are not affected by light-path blockages, since they are always served by WiFi. ③ As for the category "LiFi only", data transmission is not available during blockages. ④ Users in the category "LiFi/WiFi" will experience one VHO when a light-path blockage occurs and another VHO when the blockage disappears. ⑤ The VHO overhead is denoted by T_{vho}. ⑥ Let k denote the type of network access. ⑦ The proportion of time that is available for LiFi to serve user u is denoted by $T_{k,u}^{LiFi}$, and regarding WiFi it is denoted by $T_{k,u}^{WiFi}$. ⑧ For different types of network access, $T_{k,u}^{LiFi}$ and $T_{k,u}^{WiFi}$ are expressed as: ... ⑨ The average throughput achieved by user u is denoted by $\bar{R}_u$, and it can be calculated as follows: ...	Sentences ①, ②, ⑤, ⑦, ⑧ and ⑨ adopt passive voice. Sentence ④ is the only sentence in active voice, because "users" are the focus of this sentence. They are not explicit in the context if omitted.

(Wu, X. & Haas, H. 2019. Load balancing for hybrid LiFi and WiFi networks: To tackle user mobility and light-path blockage. *IEEE Transactions on Communications*, 68(3): 1675–1683.)

Chapter 3
Describing Methods

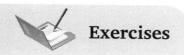

Exercises

I. Please distinguish the three steps in this figure description and summarize the main information of each step.

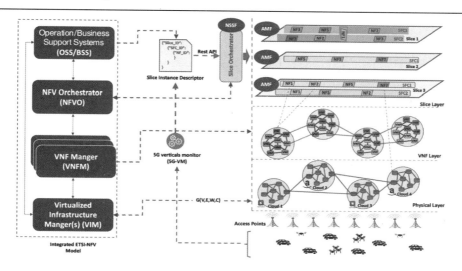

Fig. 1. Global architecture of the proposed solution.

Excerpt	Comment
Fig. 1 depicts the architecture overview suggested in this paper. We have divided the architecture into three layers, as it integrates the ETSI-NFV model and the 3GPP entities to enable the monitoring, selection and creation process of the virtual instances. The physical layer consists of a set of servers and routers. In this layer, the servers are grouped into a set of data centers that communicate between themselves through the physical network. A set of routers would be used as connectors for connecting different data centers. In the NFV model, this layer refers to the NFV infrastructure (NFVI) and would be controlled by the Virtualized Infrastructure Manager (VIM) presented in the same figure. The VNF layer consists of a set of virtual network functions (VNFs) created on top of the servers. Each VNF is dedicated to one or many functionalities during the forwarding of different data traffics. The VNF layer is managed by the VNF Manager (VNFM) that ensures the life-cycle management of all VNF instances spreading over multiple administrative domains. The slice layer, which runs on top of the VNF layer, consists of a set of slices that are dedicated to different services, e.g., health-care and connected cars. The traffic in each slice is routed thanks to service function chaining (SFC), where each traffic in the slice would be forwarded using a predefined order. Each slice is formed by ingress, egress nodes, as	

(Continued)

Excerpt	Comment
well as a set of intermediate nodes. At the reception of different packets at the ingress node, which is also called classifier, the SFC of those packets would be identified, and then the traffic would be forwarded according to that specified SFC. It is noticed that the AMF is considered the classifier in the 3GPP standardization as it is the shared entity between the control plane and the data plane. For instance, in the case of connected car management that belong to the URLLC category, a slice can be comprised of more than one SFC inside a given network infrastructure. While the first SFC could be dedicated to the monitoring and control plane information, the second SFC could be used for applying different management actions i.e., the data plane. In the following work, only the core network, (CN) part is considered, while the radio part was not studied. However, the proposed solution can be also used to deploy RAN slices or RAN/CN slices if the RAN part is an NF on top of the cloud/data-center.	

(Addad, R. A., Bagaa, M., Taleb, T., Dutra, D. L. C. & Flinck, H. 2019. Optimization model for cross-domain network slices in 5G networks. *IEEE Transactions on Mobile Computing, 19*(5): 1156–1169.)

II. Please distinguish the three moves in this excerpt from the Methods section. This text contains both active and passive voice patterns. Are all of them the right choices?

Excerpt	Comment
In this section the desired evolution of the disturbance-free model (5) will be obtained with the use of a reaching law-based control strategy. In particular, we used a generalization of Gao's seminal reaching law for the case of relative degree two sliding variables since such a strategy has been shown to provide better dynamical properties of the system than its relative degree one equivalent [32]. The considered reaching law is expressed in the following way (12) where $s_m(k)$ is the relative degree two sliding variable (8) and $\varepsilon>0$, $1>q>0$ are the design parameters. The objective of this strategy is to drive the system representative point to a narrow vicinity of the sliding hyperplane and to ensure that the hyperplane is crossed in each step. We obtain the control signal which satisfies these properties by substituting (10) into the left-hand side of reaching law (12) and solving the obtained equation for $u_m(k)$. Then, the control signal has the following form (13) In formerly published literature [32] several advantageous properties of reaching law (12) have been proven. Two of those properties will now be quoted.	

(Latosinski, P. & Bartoszewicz, A. 2020. Model reference DSMC with a relative degree two switching variable. *IEEE Transactions on Automatic Control. 66*(4): 1749–1755.)

Chapter 4
Reporting Results

4.1 Lead-in

Answer the following questions.

1. What do you expect to find in the Results section?

2. Do you think the Results section should include the unexpected results?

3. How do you think the Results section should be structured?

A majority of people would like to read the Results section before deciding whether to read the whole article. This is because the Results section is the core of a research article, and all the other sections help explain the results. In the Introduction, the authors provide background information, indicate a research gap in the field and propose research questions or hypotheses that are expected to be answered by the research, and then the Methods section explains what or how the authors do to get the results, which are subsequently presented in the Results section and interpreted and explained in the Discussion section.

The Results section summarizes and reports what you have obtained and observed (Boxman & Boxman, 2020) through the methods mentioned in Chapter 3. It is expected to describe the findings in an objective way.

Despite that this book follows IMRD model, we should be aware that not all journals are strictly structured like this. Some journals would integrate the Methods section and Results section or Results section and Discussion section. For amateur researchers, it is suggested that they fully understand the differences between the Results and Discussion sections and can use the moves and steps in these two sections with flexibility.

In some IEEE journals, the Results section and the Discussion section seem alike at first glance, both with subsections stating the results, figures and tables reporting the statistics, and algorithms proving theorems. However, these two sections serve different functions. The Results section is relatively more objective; to be specific, it mainly serves to report what we have obtained and observed, while the Discussion section tends to focus more on the interpretation of the results.

The key skill for a clear Results section is to "decide what results are representative, and then to organize them in a sequence that highlights the answers to the aims, hypotheses or questions that you set yourself at the beginning of the paper" (Wallwork, 2011, p. 233). The

Chapter 4
Reporting Results

Results section is usually structured in a logical sequence, such as a chronological sequence of the results got from the previous method, or a hierarchical order. A hierarchically ordered section places the results according to their relative salience, such as from general to specific, whole to part, and so on (van Dijk, 1977).

Based on Basturkmen (2009), Glasman-Deal (2009), Kanoksilapatham (2005; 2015) and Wallwork (2011), a Results section in IEEE journals can be composed of three basic moves, and there are a few steps within each move:

- **Move 1: Contextualizing results**

    Step 1 Providing background information

    Step 2 Listing procedures or methodological techniques

    Step 3 Stating research questions or hypothesis

    Step 4 Describing aims and purposes

    Step 5 Referring to previous research

    Step 6 Summarizing main results

- **Move 2: Reporting results (obligatory)**

    Results shown by figures or tables.

- **Move 3: Summarizing results**

    Step 1 Instantiating results

    Step 2 Invalidating results

4.2 Contextualizing Results

In the beginning of the Results section, you can state the overview of the research purposes, questions, hypotheses or methods. By briefly reviewing what you have done in the previous sections, you are getting prepared to fill the research gap and solve the research problems with solid statistics or evidence.

4.2.1 Providing Background Information

You can provide some background information about your methods in the beginning of the Results section. For example,

Excerpt	Comments
① We perform Monte-Carlo simulations to evaluate the proposed techniques. ② The one-stage nML detector is based on Algorithm 1 with a termination threshold and step size $k = 0.01$. For the two-stage nML detector, we let the constant $c = 1.3$ in (38). ③ We first consider the single cell scenario to compare detector performance. ④ Then we take the multicell scenario into account.	The authors review the methodology and some parameters used in the research in Sentences ① and ②. Sentences ③ and ④ briefly introduce the two scenario that will be presented in the Results section.

(Choi, J., Mo, J. & Heath, R. W. 2016. Near maximum-likelihood detector and channel estimator for uplink multiuser massive MIMO systems with one-bit ADCs. *IEEE Transactions on Communications*, 64(5): 2005–2018.)

The following sentences can help you to write a brief beginning of the Results section:

* *In this section, we discuss the performance of...through a series of experiments conducted with...data whereby... We first investigate... Then, we investigate...and... using...*
* *In this section, we present the experimental framework used to test our approach and the corresponding results. First, we analyze... Then, we present...*
* *We perform...simulations to evaluate the proposed techniques. The...detector is based on Algorithm x with... For the...detector, we let... We first consider the...scenario to compare... Then we take the...into account.*
* *In this section, we first perform a comprehensive validation of our...approach introduced in Section x. Then, we compare our...technique with the existing specialized...techniques. Finally, we prove the utility of our approach for applications such as...and...*
* *In order to verify the properties of the proposed..., an inventory system with...were performed.*

4.2.2 Listing Procedures or Methodological Techniques

You can also provide detailed information about the apparatus, experimental parameters that are important for your readers to re-generate the experiment and results.

Chapter 4
Reporting Results

Excerpt	Comments
Experimental Results We now evaluate our illumination, albedo and surface height estimation methods on both synthetic and real data. We implement our methods in Matlab and run experiments on a MacBook Pro 2.7 GHz with 16 GB RAM. To construct and solve the linear system of equations required to estimate surface height takes around 1 second. The alternating optimisation to estimate illumination also takes around 1 second. Albedo estimation is the most computationally expensive part of our method, with the nonlinear optimisation taking around 20 seconds. For synthetic data, we render images of the Stanford bunny with a physically-based reflectance model appropriate for smooth dielectrics (Fig. 6a). For diffuse reflectance we use the Wolff model. For specular reflectance we use Fresnel-modulated perfect mirror reflection. We vary the light source direction over and We simulate the effect of polarisation according to (3), (6) and (43) with varying polariser angle, add Gaussian noise of standard deviation, saturate and quantise to 8 bits. Illumination is modelled as a dense aggregate of 1,000 point sources, distributed around **s**, and we aggregate the polarisation fields over these sources. We estimate a polarisation image for each noise/illumination condition and use this as input. In order to evaluate our method on real world images, we capture two datasets using a Canon EOS-1D X with an Edmund Optics glass linear polarising filter. The first dataset is captured in a dark room using a Lowel Prolight. We experiment with both known and unknown lighting. For known lighting, the approximate position of the light source is measured and to calibrate for unknown light source intensity and surface albedo, we use the method in Section 5.4 to compute the length of the light source vector, fixing its direction to the measured one. The second dataset is captured outdoors on a sunny day using natural illumination.	After building models for estimating surface height from a single polarization image by a large sparse system of linear equations in the previous few sections, the Results section describes the devices used to conduct the experiments. The first paragraph provides details about the parameters to re-generate the experimental results. Then in the second paragraph the authors describe several different models used for different data. In the last paragraph, the authors describe how they verify their method. Through these three steps, we would expect to find whether the results can prove their models in the following section.

(Smith, W. A., Ramamoorthi, R. & Tozza, S. 2018. Height-from-polarisation with unknown lighting or albedo. *IEEE Transactions on Pattern Analysis and Machine Intelligence*, 41(12): 2875–2888.)

We can use the following sentences to list the procedures.

* *In this section we present the numerical results obtained through... For comparison to..., we assume a...scheme where...*
* *The methodology presented in Sections III and IV was implemented to... The experimental setup is based on... Using..., we were able to...// ...were preprocessed using... The machine was studied as a...by considering... The model was developed using a combination of...and...described in Fig. x. The validity of the model was evaluated by...*
* *In Sections II and III, we have assumed that... However, ... Fortunately, state-of-the-art...present a...which is... Consequently, assuming...does not significantly bias the estimation performance. Should the...be..., ...can still be applied using...on...*
* *In the research, three different test categories comprised by different types of content were defined: The...category, consisting of...and...content, the... category and the...category. Moreover, two sets of...were defined. A x case, denoted as x set 1, and a y case, denoted as y set 2. For the x case, ... For the y case, ... Our model was tested against two anchors, the first one being the...anchor and the second one being the...anchor.*
* *All the scripting for the model has been done using...running on Intel...CPU...GHz with...GB RAM. The details about the datasets employed, performance parameters and the existing state-of-the-art models are given below.*
* *We evaluated our...method on... We first defined...as described below (see Section x-1) and tested various features extracted from...as described further below (see Section x-2) before conducting our main experiments.*
* *We now evaluate our...and...methods on both synthetic and real data. We implement our methods in Matlab and run experiments on...(device). To construct and solve the...equations required to...// ...is the most computationally expensive part of our method, with the...taking around...seconds.*
* *For the experiments presented in this section we used a selection of data sets with... Among the data sets used are the...data set [reference], data sets of randomly sampled data of different dimensionality, data sets of...features of different sizes obtained by sampling from the...data set as well as a data set of...features extracted from...*
* *Firstly, to characterize the...of our proposed...solution obtained using Algorithm x, we compare its performance with the optimal solution obtained by the...method, and then with the three other described baselines. Since the...method..., it is...; hence, we carry out the comparison... We randomly generate...*
* *Several...experiments have been performed...(condition) to collect estimate...parameters and to compare the results from the simulation. The experiments include the following parameters...*

Chapter 4
Reporting Results

4.2.3 Stating Research Questions or Hypotheses

You can restate the research questions or hypotheses you have raised in the Introduction. The following sentence structures can help you to organize this step.

> * *Since our model is data-driven and..., and given the abundance of datasets, we wanted to answer questions such as..., ..., and... As a result, we performed experiments on...number different datasets, explained in Section x, which enabled us to understand our model in depth.*
> * *Typically, the first question considered when dealing with...concerns...*
> * *Our hypothesis is that...can be tackled by... Moreover, ...could help obtain better results by... More experimentation is needed to validate these hypotheses.*

4.2.4 Describing Aims and Purposes

You can also restate the aims or purposes of your research in the beginning of the Results section to keep reminding your readers of what you are doing and why you are doing so. The following sentence structures can be signals to your readers about what you are going to present.

> * *Our final purpose is to obtain a...that... We compared our method with previous methods that can...[references]. We used...to train..., and...to evaluate...performance. We determined...as the...value of...in (algorithm) by 2-fold cross-validation. All the...methods used in our comparison used...as an initial state.*
> * *The objective was to..., i.e., to... To solve..., we used... The covariance x of the initial state was...allowing each angle to be off by about y degree.*
> * *The goal of our experiments is to validate the theory, by showing that..., and that by adapting...to...we can better exploit architectures of... To this end, we first compare...with...on several standard benchmark datasets using different networks architecture, and highlight a few key properties.*
> * *To test the effect of the...to model the...as in (algorithm x) in Section x, we compare the results of the...solution to calculate...using the...expression versus using the...expression of...*
> * *To investigate the performance of the proposed framework presented in Section x, ...have been conducted using...software, i.e...*

4.2.5 Referring to Previous Research

You can bring about your results by briefly comparing or contrasting with previous research, for example:

> * *Many papers have shown that...[references]// ...is a difficult task, one of the main*

> challenges being the impossibility of...For example, ...// ...is even more problematic for...used in [references]. When dealing with..., possible solutions include...
> * ...has been used in the literature with good results [references], however, it can be challenging to... In...we used the approach of...
> * ...is used in a large number of both research and industry projects (e.g., [references]) and is widely used in..., in part due to...// ...also is used by other well-known open-source projects, such as...[references].
> * While...give insight into..., they usually do not provide guidance to practitioners for... More relevant for practical applications are research efforts that aim at...[references] have shown that...

4.2.6 Summarizing Main Results

It is also a good choice to summarize the main results at the beginning of the Results section.

Excerpt	Comment
We demonstrated the data proxy's utility in maximizing data richness and reducing resource use in the context of our IoT architecture by optimizing the QoD for a target cost and optimizing the cost for a target QoD. Further, we showed that the optimal sampling arrangement varies with sensor costs and QoD type.	The authors briefly introduce what they have done and what results they have obtained.

(Siegel, J. E., Kumar, S. & Sarma, S. E. 2017. The future Internet of Things: Secure, efficient, and model-based. *IEEE Internet of Things Journal*, 5(4): 2386–2398.)

You can refer to the following sentences to summarize your results.

> * *This section presents the results of the experimental evaluation of the proposed...detection model across different case studies.*
> * This section summarizes the...test results. It also provides an analysis with a focus on a comparison with the...test results.
> * In this section, we present the numerical results of our algorithms detecting...in Section x-C.
> * We demonstrated the utility of...in...in the context of our...architecture by... Further, we showed that...
> * In this section we show...achieved with different...when... In particular we compare our results with the performances we achieve: a) with...and b) with...
> * In this section, the parameters of...models are computed using... Subsequently, we present experimental and simulation results to show...
> * In this section we are going to analyze the results obtained with our approach by comparing them with an exhaustive experimentation to determine... In the exhaustive search we used...
> * This section is divided into 3 different parts. First, we describe how we... Second, we

compare our approach with...methods. Third, we evaluate the performance of...

* *To better show the potential of...we perform... We first evaluate the...in Section x-A. Afterwards in Section x-B we discuss the..., the...and the throughput performance in... Finally, in Section x-C, we consider the scenario of...*
* *In the following, we demonstrate the advantages of...and...based on... In particular, we evaluate the effects of...// ...is analyzed in two scenarios: a...versus a... The...results clearly outline...*
* *In this section we will extensively evaluate our...algorithm. We both compare it to other...methods, as well as evaluate the effect of important design and parameter choices. We use three datasets for evaluation...*
* *...results are presented to evaluate the performance of our proposed...strategy, referred to as...*
* *In this section, we first validate our...results using...simulations. We consider a network with... In Fig. x, we plot the...for the...scheme. We observe that... Also note that Fig. x matches with our...illustration of...in Fig. y, which plots the...in Theorem x, and the...in Theorem y.*

4.3 Reporting Results

Reporting what you have found is the main function of the Results section. It is the only obligatory move in this section (Williams, 1999), as it states the main findings or results that this research has revolved around.

The results are usually organized from general to specific. You can make a claim about the overall results in the beginning, and illustrate the specific results one by one. You can also start from the most important findings or the results that underlie or lead to the more important ones (Glasman-Deal, 2009).

Usually, you can just state your results directly, or you can use some cue words or sentences to remind your readers as the following.

Excerpt	Comment
Two illustrative examples are presented in this section. In both cases the differential game corresponding to the problem associated with the agents is solved using Theorem 2 and for the collision avoidance functions (6) the parameter c=1 has been used.	The authors simply present the main findings of the two examples.

(Mylvaganam, T., Sassano, M. & Astolfi, A. 2017. A differential game approach to multi-agent collision avoidance. *IEEE Transactions on Automatic Control*, *62*(8): 4229–4235.)

* *Results show...*
* *This section provides performance results for... Individual results for the new features of..., and...are first reported. Then, ...and...are compared as a whole with respect to..., and... This is done by comparing a realization of..., and a model of... In this model, ...has been extended in a straightforward manner to deal with...*

4.3.1 Results Shown by Figures or Tables

The results are usually presented in the form of figures or tables. You need to describe these figures or tables by summarizing the main information, indicating changes, or making comparison and contrast.

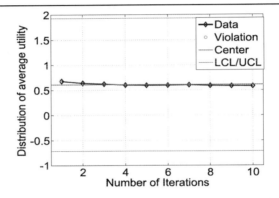

Fig. 10. Normalized average utility of the associations for D = 50.

Excerpt	Comment
①Fig. 10 shows the control chart of the utility distribution of the associations in the proposed AHP based matching approach, where the utility is well-balanced, and there is no violation, and the normalized average utility of the associations at each iteration is close to the central line. ②At each iteration, the IoT device density at each Fog device increases and when the IoT device density is much lower, the performance gain in terms of utility is quite higher than the average line and tends to upper control limit (UCL). ③As the IoT device density in the network increases (i.e., $|D|$) the normalized average utility per Fog device slimly tends toward lower control limit (LCL) which is expected due to externalities. ④However, none of the distributions violates the upper (UCL) and lower control limit (LCL) despite the negative effect of externalities at higher IoT device density.	Sentence ① is a summary of the key information in Fig. 10. Sentences ② and ③ describe how the different schemes change according to the number of iterations. The description focuses on the trends of changes. Sentence ④ is the interpretation of the results. It also serves as a summary of the results.

(Abedin, S. F., Alam, M. G. R., Kazmi, S. A., Tran, N. H., Niyato, D. & Hong, C. S. 2018. Resource allocation for ultra-reliable and enhanced mobile broadband IoT applications in fog network. *IEEE Transactions on Communications, 67*(1): 489–502.)

Chapter 4
Reporting Results

The beginning of a figure/table description usually contains "a location element and a brief summary of what can be found in a visual display of information" (Swales & Feak, 2012, p. 147). For example, *Table x summarizes the results of different schemes with different variables.*

A location element can guide your readers through reading, especially when they need to combine your text with the visual display. The first sentence in a figure description serves as an orientation as well as an overview of the figure.

Excerpt	Comment
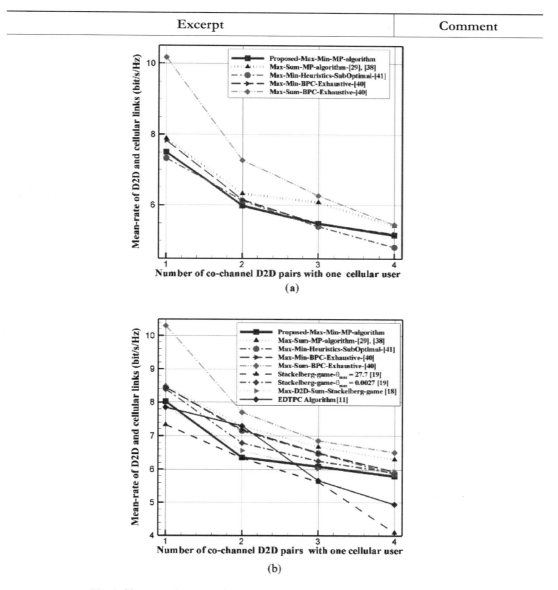 Fig. 4. Mean-rate in terms of the number of co-channel D2D pairs for TDU=2, 4 per RDU. (a) For TDU=2. (b) For TDU=4.	

(Continued)

Excerpt	Comment
① The results are depicted in Fig. 4 in terms of the number of co-channels D2D pairs with cellular user and 2 and 4 TDUs for each RDU. ② Clearly, the system mean-rate decreases by increasing the number of co-channels D2D pairs. ③ Since the interference of D2D users imposed on the performance of cellular users is limited and QoS requirements provided by the cellular users are met, increasing the number of D2D pairs maximizes the spectral efficiency and consequently the network sum-rate. ④ Moreover, increasing the number of TDUs for each RDU in order to make more choices, increases the network mean-rate as well. ⑤ As a general rule, the achieved mean-rate of the proposed max-min MP algorithm is less than that of the max-sum MP algorithm and the max-sum BPC exhaustive search. ⑥ However, it converges to the result of the max-sum algorithm by increasing the number of co-channels D2D pairs with a smaller slope compared to the max-sum algorithm. ⑦ The reason is that the purpose of the max-sum problem is to maximize the sum-rate of the whole network and it does not concern individual users, while the max-min problem searches the best answer for the case all users' rates satisfy a minimum value constraint and that value would be maximized. ⑧ Consequently, the performance of both algorithms leads to the same result by increasing the number of active users. ⑨ On the other hand, the proposed MP algorithm achieves 90% of the max-min BPC exhaustive search performance in the worst case and about 97% in the best case by reducing the order of complexity from $O(N^4L^N\log(NL))$ to $O(N^2L2K^2))$. ⑩ It almost achieved 100% of the max-min heuristics algorithm in the best case and 92% in the worst case by reducing the order of complexity from $O(N^3L^3)$ to $O(N^2L^2K^2)$. ⑪ Both of these compared algorithms are binary while the proposed algorithm works on K-ary values. ⑫ Therefore, in the average 6.5% loss is negligible compared to the above-mentioned complexity reduction that the proposed algorithm attains in comparison with the centralized schemes. ⑬ In comparison with the two other distributed game-theoretic schemes, it is clear that the performance of our proposed scheme is close to both works in [18] and [19].	Sentence ① contains a location element and a summary of the figure. Sentence ② presents the most significant result, and it begins with "clearly" as a signal. Next, an explanation of this result is given in Sentences ③ and ④. Sentence ⑤ moves to another aspect of the results by stating a general rule, followed by some supplementary information in Sentence ⑥. Then, this result is explained in Sentence ⑦, which leads to further results in Sentence ⑧. Sentence ⑨ is signaled by "on the other hand", which indicates a different aspect of the results. Then Sentence ⑩ provides more details, followed by an inference in Sentences ⑪ and ⑫. Sentence ⑬ makes a comparison of the proposed scheme with other schemes and makes a claim about the result.

Chapter 4
Reporting Results

(Continued)

Excerpt	Comment
⑭ However, the convergence of our proposed scheme is guaranteed and the power allocation is fair, compared to the two other schemes; these schemes try to keep the performance of some users near to the QoS level and this leads to achieving a Nash-equilibrium point which is far from the optimality. ⑮ The other challenge of these schemes is the determination of the optimal pricing factor. ⑯ The EDTPC algorithm proposed in [11] also has almost the same performance compared to the proposed max-min MP algorithm, while it is more sensitive to the number of co-channel users and minimum SINR threshold.	In Sentence ⑭, the authors make a positive evaluation about their proposed scheme after the detailed description above. Then, this claim is supported by the evaluation of other schemes in Sentences ⑮ and ⑯.

(Rashed, S. K., Asvadi, R., Rajabi, S., Ghorashi, S. A. & Martini, M. G. 2020. Power allocation for D2D communications using max-min message-passing algorithm. *IEEE Transactions on Vehicular Technology*, *69*(8): 8443–8458.)

From the above examples we can see that a figure description has a clear structure like this: general→specific→general. In the beginning, a location statement and summary of the main findings or the key information in the figure is necessary. This is the most general claim made through the observation of the figure, and needs to be supported and expanded with details in the following sentences. While developing the claim, details about the data are needed. These details are organized according to some logical orders such as cause and effect, compare and contrast, etc. More structures of figure description can be found in the following sentences:

* *Results for...and...tasks are summarized in Tables x and y, respectively.*
* *Table x shows...for each method, and we highlight in bold the best-A and best-B method between...and..., and between...and... A sample visual result is shown in Fig. x.*
* *The results in Table x illustrate. // ...is added...with a...that... For..., we input... The... can handle..., which... It outperforms...on..., whether...*
* *The...presented in the previous sections is summarized in Table x in terms of...for the...configurations.*
* *For..., we use...for...// ...is simulated and added to...before running it through a...method. // ...results are reported in Table x.*
* *The performance of...is tested by...(method). Table x compares...and... cases. Positive numbers show... For the...configuration, ...shows an average...gain of x%. Since...is applied only to..., the gains are lower for the configurations that... For..., the gain is y%, and for..., which..., the gain is z%.*

* *The...are summarized in Fig. x. These results clearly demonstrate..., as well as...This...is due to... This might raise the question of..., on the other hand... We will use this question as an example of how to take the presented...one step further, ...*
* *In order to examine the impact of..., we measured... This measure is often used in the context of...as it describes... Figs. xa and xb show the results of this evaluation for...and..., respectively.*
* *Fig. x shows... As expected, ... Increasing...does not change... Thus, it may not be necessarily suitable to..., as it does not directly improve...while it may degrade... Fig. x also shows that... Therefore, ...*
* *Fig. x depicts..., where the number of...is...and the number of...is... The...is growing exponentially where... Therefore, we consider a...for comparing our proposed approach with...*
* *Fig. x shows our...results, the...values, along with...results. The...is created by fusing the...with the... The fusion is carried out by...step and... As in practical scenarios, the...outputs are clipped to..., as are the... Our results better remove...compared with..., and details are better reconstructed over the...content. We note that, at...levels, there is a...effect, which creates... These are created by..., but are more salient in our result...as it is... The higher..., the larger... This makes...vary from...to..., randomly, and causes..., rather than a linear one, which is modeled by...*
* *The...results for each category of...are shown in Fig. x in the form of... The...are also plotted on the same graph using a second vertical axis. Note that the scales for the two vertical axes in these plots are independently selected, and thus no direct connection between the...and...plots are demonstrated.*
* *The results are depicted in terms of...and...in Figs. x(a) and x(b), respectively. It is clear that... In Fig. x(a), a...relation is seen between... and... However, by increasing..., ...decreases. Thus, the trade-off between...and...is obvious in Fig. x(a). On the other hand, the results confirm the fair performance of the proposed...algorithm which... The fairness performance is better compared to...which... In Fig. x(b), the difference between...and...increases with... This result shows the effect of...in the context of...*

Usually, you will have more than one figure or table that should be arranged in the most logical order for your readers, and each figure or table should contain some key findings and the supportive details. The results should be able to support your hypothesis or answer your research questions you raised in the Introduction (Wallwork, 2011). Then you can leave the other results in the next subsection.

Chapter 4
Reporting Results

4.4 Summarizing Results

Apart from the obligatory report of main findings, you can also interpret your results with more details.

4.4.1 Instantiating Results

You can point out what your findings have proven, how they support your hypotheses or answer your research questions, with the following sentences.

* We have assessed..., showing that... In addition, we have been able to...by... This hints in the direction that our design requirement for parallelization is met.
* In Section x, we show that..., for some..., such that the...is achieved. The proof of this result involved proving that... In practice, for..., we have to decide on a tradeoff between...and... In particular, we can..., and then...
* The robustness of the proposed...is verified in two different scenarios, namely, ...and...
* Our approach achieves a good performance in terms of...
* First, we discuss the effect of...upon the proposed... On the one hand, if..., ... On the other hand, if..., ... In this paper, the...parameter is selected to lie within the range..., and the proposed...with...has essentially consistent estimation performance and higher estimation accuracy than existing..., as shown in the later simulation. Second, we study the effect of the...upon the proposed...
* In this paper, the...parameter and the...factor are selected to lie within the ranges...and...respectively based on the above discussions. The recommendations regarding parameter ranges are specific to the...study presented in this paper, and perhaps other parameter ranges are more appropriate in other situations. Fortunately, our experience has indicated that the proposed...with the suggested parameter ranges exhibit good estimation performance in many contexts.
* The losses caused by...in...scenarios are almost negligible, as we can see in Fig. x. In particular the figure shows that the...approach is characterized by...for..., but it starts to achieve similar or better performances than the...for both...and... If we apply the...according to the...approach, then performances increase greatly for both algorithms, arriving to almost optimal performances with the...
* It can be clearly seen that the difference in...and...between...and...is small. On..., this gap is further reduced and the performance is approximately the same. Moreover, the...increases the computational complexity for... It is worth noting that...
* Our analysis in this paper is based on...assumption. To better understand the utility of

> this..., we compare the...with...whereby...
> * As for all...methods, the predominant cause of failure is...in the form of..., since... This issue is amplified since... In contrast, ...allows to..., and thereby...
> * We explain this behavior as follows: Assuming that..., ...is required to... However, when..., for example, leads to.... Therefore, ... Effectively, ...and...goes hand in hand with...
> * We have seen that both...methods have pros and cons... // ...requires more computational resources than..., but... The reason why...did not reliably succeed in...is that..., which is largely a result of..., an example of which is given in Fig. x.

4.4.2 Invalidating Results

Sometimes, you would get results that are out of your expectation or you may have encountered some difficulties or problems. How to deal with the unexpected results or problems is also one part of results interpretation. You are not supposed to just ignore those unwanted results or problems unless you are sure that they are insignificant. Failing to mention those unexpected results or problems may suggest that you are not professional enough in the field to identify and explain those results. In addition, mentioning them provides you an essential element in the Discussion section: directions or suggestions for future research (Glasman-Deal, 2009).

You can use the following sentences to justify your explanation about the results.

> * As discussed in Section x, the different...specifications, e.g., ...and..., may have a direct impact on... Indeed, as previously mentioned, different...may change how the...is perceived and introduce different... Thus, it is critical that during...experiments, researchers specify both the...and the... Moreover, there is still a lack of...studies that allow researchers to better understand the impact of the...features on the...assessment.
> * Results presented for the...models in the previous subsections were obtained employing... The performances of...are reported in Table x...does not fail but consistently performs worse than... This suggests that... The results do not provide enough evidence for... This might suggest that... Note that... might affect...as well, thus, ...
> * As shown in Fig. x, neither...nor...perform well, because the former ignores...and the latter fail to...
> * From the visual results in Fig. x, we see that...do not manage to generate convincing...results about... These models fail to...
> * One interesting aspect to notice in Table x is that for problems with..., the heuristic seems to fail when...
> * We have not observed significant..., likely due to...
> * The proposed...model will fail when...

Chapter 4
Reporting Results

4.5 Language Focus

4.5.1 Dealing with Graphs

In most cases, IEEE journal articles present their results in figures, graphs and tables. We can use both nouns and verbs to describe the changes, and also use some adjectives and adverbs to modify the extent and speed of the changes.

1) Describing Changes

One important element that can be visualized is the trends, such as the changes of results or the effects of changing different variables on the results. Different expressions to describe changes can be seen in the following sentences:

* The rate of...<u>increases</u> by increasing...
* Fig. x shows that increasing...may <u>increase/decrease</u>...probability, depending on...
* For..., increasing...<u>improves</u>...
* If we apply..., then performances <u>increase</u> greatly for...
* With every (1 m/s) increase in speed, the gap between the proposed method and...<u>increases</u> by about x%.
* The results plotted in Fig. x show clearly that...<u>increases</u> linearly along with...
* As...<u>increases</u>, ...become more (comparative)...
* The further we <u>increase</u>..., the larger is the performance gap between...and...
* We observed that, by reducing..., we <u>increase</u>...
* Additionally, if we <u>increase</u> the number of..., then we get...as can be seen from Fig. x.
* Fig. x. presents the improvements in...as the number of...<u>are increased</u> in the proposed...scheme. It is shown that with this increase, the number of...<u>increases</u> and this also provides a better...due to...
* We observe that...also follow the similar trend, i.e., they <u>increase</u> with...and <u>decrease</u> with...
* When...<u>increases</u> from...to...in the case of..., ...<u>drops</u> from...to... Meanwhile, ...has a <u>decrease</u> of x% in..., and...has a <u>decrease</u> of y%.
* The (green) dots in Fig. x show...; they <u>decline</u> almost linearly relative to...
* This...is expected to continue to <u>decline</u> as...
* As shown in Fig. x, ...suddenly <u>drops</u> when..., which indicates...
* We also observe significant <u>jumps</u> in...when...
* The increasing..., combined with..., leads to an <u>increase</u> in terms of...
* Noteworthy is the steep <u>increase</u> in...

* The rate of...is <u>smaller</u> than...
* Fig. x plots...and shows a monotonic <u>increase</u> of...
* For..., we see a polynomial <u>increase</u> of...
* The slight <u>increase</u> of...is expected due to...
* Fig. x shows the estimated..., confirming the <u>drop</u> in...

2) Describing Extent of Change

You can also use some adjectives and adverbs to describe the extent of changes, for example:

* Given that the field has seen <u>significant advances</u> in the last years, we do think it is more meaningful to report..., which...
* For..., increasing the density of...might lead to <u>a significant decline</u> of...
* The top plot in Fig. x shows that <u>a substantial decrease</u> in...is experienced by ...
* As can be seen in Fig. x, for..., ...do not introduce <u>a significant degradation</u> in quality, while...is observed.
* We also observe <u>significant jumps</u> in...when...
* After sufficient number of samples, there is no further <u>significant reduction</u> in the gap between...and...
* This also explains the <u>huge increase</u> in...by...
* Noteworthy is the <u>steep increase</u> in... for..., illustrating that...
* From the figure, we can see that...provides <u>substantial gains</u> over...
* This causes <u>a very slight decrease</u> in...because...
* In Fig. x, we observe <u>a very small increase</u> in...
* We see <u>the biggest increase</u> in the average...scores when...
* When...is too large, it prevents...from..., jeopardizing...and causing <u>a drastic increase</u> in error.
* For..., we see <u>a polynomial increase</u> of...in...
* As shown in Fig. x, the proposed method can <u>significantly increase</u>...over..., especially for...
* With our default search set..., ...nearly always succeeds for..., then <u>drops sharply</u> to...
* It is evident from the figure that...<u>considerably reduces</u>...
* ...<u>considerably improves</u>...
* ...started from x and <u>largely increased</u> as...
* In..., using...could <u>dramatically increase</u>...with minimal loss in...
* The...error of the...model parameters <u>decrease monotonically</u> with the number of...in Fig. x.

3) Describing Speed of Change

You can also use some adjectives and adverbs to describe the speed of changes, for example:

* It is worth noticing how...obtained by...<u>rapidly decrease</u> with the number of users in the scenario, because of...
* As shown in Fig. x, ...<u>suddenly drops</u> when...is from x to y, which indicates...
* ...size was <u>extended progressively</u> from x to y, and for each scenario...were <u>gradually increased</u> from x% to y%.
* It is seen from... that the effect of...on is <u>gradually reduced</u> as...increases.
* The results plotted in Fig. x show clearly that...<u>increases linearly</u> along with the number of...
* We proposed a...strategy to <u>gently change</u> the...process.
* This may be considered <u>a moderate loss</u> when compared to...
* The effect of...may be modeled as <u>a slow large-scale fading effect</u> since...
* Regarding..., we observe <u>a quick increase</u> concerning...
* ...allows <u>a steady reduction</u> in...and enables...

4) Describing Approximation in Changes

Sometimes we can use approximation expressions to describe values, numbers that are not an integer or close to a certain number.

* ...is <u>nearly</u> constant above x, showing that...
* Table x shows that on average, the...method reduces...rate by <u>approximately</u> x%.
* Compared with..., ...of our scheme is <u>approximately</u> x%–y% lower.
* Our scheme shows <u>approximately the same</u> performance as...and is <u>up to</u> x% better than...
* We find that the...approaches achieve accuracies <u>nearly</u> identical to those achieved by..., showing that...
* ...<u>almost</u> triples the run times shown in Fig. x.
* Performance was even better for..., where <u>almost</u> a quarter of...
* For..., ...and...have <u>almost</u> the same performance at (condition)...
* The data convincingly show that the...is achieving...that is <u>at least</u> x%.
* For..., a value <u>close to</u> x indicates...
* For..., the...effect degrades the...performance by <u>about</u> x dB.
* ...made the...swing in a radius of <u>about</u> x cm.
* The covariance x of the initial state was...allowing each angle to be off by <u>about</u> y degree.

* ...achieved <u>about</u> x percent success on average.
* Both...yield predictors of...with accuracies <u>over</u> x%.
* We construct...feature data set by randomly sampling a data set of <u>over</u> x million...features extracted from...
* As can be seen, ...ratios in the...scenarios always remained <u>under</u> a tolerable x% loss, which means...
* Where there are <u>more than</u> x users, the proposed method achieves the highest throughput.
* Comparing to Fig. x, where the...is <u>less than</u> about..., the...from Fig. y is about...
* It is advisable to divide...into groups of..., each with <u>fewer than</u> x...

4.5.2 Compare and Contrast

While reporting results, we always need to compare and contrast either with previous research, or within your results.

* We present...tests on different...datasets, and <u>compare</u> the results of...<u>and</u> of...
* <u>Compared to</u>..., ...was faster when using a...approach.
* We <u>compare</u> in Figure x the...obtained using our...scheme (Figure x-a) and the other methods (Figure x-b, c, d).
* If we <u>compare</u> the reported results to the results in Table x, we see that most methods achieve consistently higher...as...gets smaller. // ...is very competitive and achieves clearly the best performance among all tested methods for the...task.
* In terms of..., the results <u>are similar as</u> in the previous section: The...architecture results in..., while the...contribute towards...when measured through...
* As seen in Table x, our...approach improves the...at...level starting from..., which includes... <u>Comparing</u>...and..., we also note with our approach an improvement of... We <u>outperform</u>...by an average of...with our version trained on...levels and we perform...when... <u>Comparing</u> the results of...and of...in Table x, for..., we see that... <u>The improvement of...is consistent with</u> that obtained in our...experiment in Table y.
* The...allows all methods <u>to perform significantly better in terms of</u>...on...compared with...
* In Fig. x, <u>a comparison between</u>...and the proposed...is illustrated when...
* <u>Similarly</u>, ...can be...along similar lines.
* The proposed method <u>is also compared with</u> the existing methods which handle...in Table x. It can be seen that the...model <u>outperforms</u> other methods for...// ...and... methods solve only...issue. This is why, not applicable (N/A) is mentioned in table for 0.1 amount of uncertainty.

* One of the key advantages of x as <u>compared with</u> y is that... This is due to the fact that..., while y just...
* While the result of the previous section shows that the proposed...provides..., it is only compared against...and thus does not... To this end, we <u>compare</u> the performance of...against...which work as follows: (i)..., and (ii)...
* The predicted...from the proposed method <u>are compared with</u>...using three evaluation indices..., ...and...
* In this section, we validate that our...method is <u>more effective at</u>...<u>compared with</u>..., and that our...further improves the performance via...
* <u>Unlike</u>...that works on..., ...and...using...and in the...domain respectively. We...for a fair comparison.
* Fig. x shows that our method produces <u>more accurate</u>...<u>than</u> a, b and c. It is interesting to see that our method <u>achieves equally good quantitative results</u> with..., but...leads to...
* Fig. x shows that our...method <u>achieves higher correspondence accuracy compared with</u>...and...on the...testing set. The consistent improvement from...to...indicates that...
* Furthermore, <u>comparing</u> Figs. x and y, we notice that...are significantly...than... This shows that our strategy...
* Fig. y <u>compares</u>...and... This figure shows that the results are more...due to... Note that...
* We <u>compare</u> the...model with...state-of-the-art...models, i.e... [references]. Since some of these models were introduced for...problems, we retrain all models on the...dataset and use open-source implementations of the authors (where available) for a fair comparison.
* To highlight the benefits of our...approach over...methods we also consider the...measurements used in Fig. x and <u>compare</u> our approach to the classical...method (see details in [reference]). This approach is chosen as <u>it is the best</u>...method which... Although the comparison could have been performed using...and more advanced methods, the competing methods would have led to <u>significantly higher</u>...costs. To apply the..., we first...

4.5.3 Describing Sequences

To make sure that your readers could follow your description of methods and also compare their results with yours, you should be able to precisely describe the time and order sequence of what you did and found (Glasman-Deal, 2009). You can use the following sentence structures.

* <u>At the beginning of</u>..., the proposed...algorithm runs...

* *The average...between...and...is relatively close <u>at the beginning</u> when...*
* *X reduces Y. Y is <u>then</u>...*
* *In particular, we can set..., <u>and then</u> compute...*
* *The master server...<u>and then</u>...*
* *A...study was <u>first</u> mentioned in [reference] <u>and then</u> presented in [reference].*
* *First, these sensors are placed at... Subsequently, these sensors are moved to...*
* *The...dataset is customary used for... only <u>after</u>...*
* *<u>After</u>...was detected, ...was used to...*
* *The effects of...became noticeable <u>after</u>...*
* *The initial work on...has been driven by..., with the aim of showing that... After this initial phase...*
* *With time, ...degraded and <u>as soon as</u> it reached..., ...was initiated.*
* *...operation starts <u>as soon as</u>...is over.*
* *In particular, it is interesting to notice how...is accomplished while providing <u>at the same time</u> higher efficiencies.*
* *...was computed for...<u>prior to</u> starting...*
* *...is presented in Fig. x, where <u>initially</u> the...value was...*
* *For..., we assume... <u>Later</u>, we evaluate...*
* *...can store energy...<u>and later</u> deliver it to...*
* *The...is significant when... <u>Meanwhile</u>, ...indicate that...*
* *<u>Lastly</u>, when we apply...we can see that...*

4.5.4 Describing Frequency

When reporting a result, it is also important to indicate how often it occurs. Without a frequency modifier, your readers may not be able to evaluate your results appropriately if they lack information about how often a particular result occurs (Glasman-Deal, 2009). Some frequency expressions can be seen in the following sentence structures.

* *...is shown to <u>always</u> act as...*
* *From Fig. x, we can observe that...<u>always</u> performs the best, and that...*
* *We observe in..., transmission between various...still <u>usually</u> succeeds at distances up to...*
* *In the design of..., ...<u>often</u> plays an important role.*
* *With <u>every</u> x m/s increase in speed, the...gap between the proposed method and...increases by about x%.*
* *The...signal could be changed <u>every</u> x m/s.*
* *The benefit of the proposed method becomes greater when...occur more <u>frequently</u>.*

> * *While providing reasonably...results, ...produces only...among all tested models. This result is expected and is observed <u>regularly</u> in [reference] with...methods.*
> * *Table x summarizes...<u>commonly</u> found in...*
> * *It is shown that...is <u>generally</u> lower than...*
> * *The performance of...is <u>generally</u> good even where...*
> * *The success rate was approximately x%; ...was <u>sometimes</u> impossible due to...*
> * *Considering..., where...conditions are dynamically changing due to..., where...will be initiated <u>every now and then</u> following...*
> * *While the effect is <u>hardly</u> visible to..., it has a severe impact on...*
> * *For..., the...model <u>never</u> ranks worse than second, but is overall close to the runner up, the...model, in this experiment.*
> * *The data convincingly show that...is achieving...that is <u>at least</u> x%.*

4.5.5 Describing Quantity

The interpretation of numbers in figures or tables depends on how you see them. Your attitude towards the numbers affects how your readers view the results. For example, if you say "As can be seen from Fig. x, results show 20% improvement in the performance", you can interpret this improvement as either a strong result "as much as 20% improvement" or a weak result "only 20% improvement" (Glasman-Deal, 2009, p. 103). You can use the following sentence structures to describe quantity.

> * *Image x contains <u>a great amount of</u>...details.*
> * *We can see that...and yet provide a <u>considerable</u> benefit in terms of...*
> * *Without..., although...gradually..., the...have relatively lower...and <u>considerable</u> higher...*
> * *Results show a <u>considerable</u> improvement between the original method and after applying...*
> * *In Fig. x we can see how... selects <u>a number of</u> beams that...*
> * *In this scenario, <u>a number of</u>..., each..., are added to...to support...*
> * *To study any of the scenario, we generate <u>a large number of</u> instances with all the parameters randomly chosen.*
> * *If x is too small, <u>a large quantity of</u> information about...is lost, which also degrades the performance of...*
> * *It can be seen that with a small and <u>moderate</u> number of...the number of... grows linearly but less than the number of...*
> * *The...improvement for...systems with...is <u>considerably less marked</u> than for an ideal...*
> * *The...exhibits abrupt changes between <u>small and large</u> values, which reflect...*

* The <u>small</u> error confirms...
* The results show a <u>substantial</u> effect for..., and a <u>noticeable</u> effect for..., see Fig. x.
* To evaluate the weakness of the...model, we examine in Fig. x a few example...that...
* In...experiments, ...algorithm produced the best solution in <u>only</u> about x% of the problems compared to y% for...
* The improvement is significant when there are <u>only</u> x% or y%...but remains noticeable when there are more.
* The...in the figure shows an example of a...that..., resulting in very <u>little</u> difference in...
* For..., all...samples used for training...were utilized for..., and accuracy changed very <u>little</u>.
* To this end, we first compare...using..., and highlight <u>a few</u> key properties.
* The...is generally measured by a...index that integrates all the possible sources of...into <u>a single</u> or <u>a few</u> values.

4.5.6 Highlight Your Finding

When you intend to emphasize the importance of your results, or to confirm the contribution of your research, you can use the following phrases to highlight your findings.

* Our method yields <u>a significant benefit</u> over the current...method.
* This is <u>a significant finding</u>, which opens a new area of...
* The new approach got <u>significant improvement</u> on...
* Another <u>important observation</u> from Fig. x, Fig. y and Fig. z is that...
* The first <u>important observation</u> is that...
* This result clearly confirms <u>the usefulness of the proposed approach</u> in terms of...
* These results <u>clearly demonstrate</u> the...impact...had on...
* <u>As expected</u>, we can clearly observe...
* We can <u>clearly see</u> that..., as shown in Table x.
* <u>It can be clearly seen that</u> the results of our method...
* <u>This result is expected</u>, as...thus...
* <u>As expected</u>, ...increases...by...
* As expected, ...<u>performs significantly better</u> with..., in particular compared to...
* As we expected to observe, when...<u>the best results are obtained</u> using...
* <u>Not that</u> we observed...

4.5.7 Impersonal Style

When reporting results, Mohammadi, et al. (2020) use the following expressions.

1. Meanwhile, <u>we compute</u> horizontal and vertical correlation coefficients for each image.

2. In Fig. 5, the histograms of BCLs for the four images <u>are illustrated</u> employing the block size of 4×4.

3. <u>Fig. 6c shows</u> the histogram of the marked encrypted image has more fluctuation than the encrypted one; however, it depicts the uniform distribution generally.

Sentence 1 makes the agent of the action explicit by using a pronoun "we", while both Sentences 2 and 3 use an impersonal style, with either a passive voice or an inanimate subject. "This usage may either reflect the author's wish to remain in the background and let his results speak for themselves, and/or because he is following his journal's requirements" (Wallwork, 2011, p. 238). This impersonal style is more likely to show objectivity in the interpretation of results.

Exercises

I. Please identify the moves and steps used in the beginning of the Results section in each of the following excerpts and underline the signalling sentences. Make comments about the functions of the sentences.

Excerpt 1	Comments
We train and test our system on a PC with an Intel Core i7-6700 k CPU, 16 GB RAM, and one Nvidia GTX 1080 graphics card with 8 GB memory. The average time cost of each training iteration is 0.25 s on GPU, and it takes 1.4 hours for 20,000 iterations to complete the whole training process. Given a reasonably large mesh from the SCAPE dataset (12,500 vertices, 24,998 triangles), it takes 26.4 s to compute the raw SH descriptors from the mesh on CPU, 0.09 s to compute the distance metric on GPU, 0.06 s to compute the saliency map on GPU, and 163.4 s to compute 30 saliency-induced embeddings from the metric on CPU. The method of [25] takes about 235.2 s for shape matching on CPU.	

(Hu, S., Shum, H. P., Aslam, N., Li, F. W. & Liang, X. 2019. A unified deep metric representation for mesh saliency detection and non-rigid shape matching. *IEEE Transactions on Multimedia, 22*(9): 2278–2292.)

Excerpt 2	Comments
The visual quality of classical images and videos is generally measured by a global quality index that (ideally) integrates all the possible sources of distortion into a single or a few values. However, as aforementioned, the sources of distortions in 360-degree videos are numerous and quite different, and their combination into a global index is far from trivial. Table I summarizes the different types of distortions commonly found in 360-degree video. We broadly categorize them as: *spatial*, i.e., those related to still image compression and can appear in both images and videos; *temporal*, i.e., those related to the temporal evolution of images and appear only on video; *stereoscopic*, i.e., those related to binocular vision; and *navigation*, i.e., those that only appear while the user navigates through the scene. The ultimate way to assess the 360-degree visual quality is through subjective tests. Such tests, however, are time consuming and expensive. Thus, objective metrics have been proposed for omnidirectional video in the past few years. However, it is quite challenging to capture all the effects that impact the QoE of 360-degree videos, and much work remains to be done in this area, in particular, with regards to perceptually optimized metrics.	

(Roberto, G. D. A., Birkbeck, N., De Simone, F., Janatra, I., Adsumilli, B. & Frossard, P. 2019. Visual distortions in 360° videos. *IEEE Transactions on Circuits and Systems for Video Technology, 30*(8): 2524–2537.)

Chapter 4
Reporting Results

II. Please identify the moves and steps in the description of the results shown in the figures and underline the signalling sentences. Make comments about the functions of the sentences.

TABLE VII

SUMMARY OF ROW COMMUNICATION FOR SET A

Statistic	CBBA	PI	Soft max
% solved	6.25	90.63	100.00
% best solutions	0.00	9.38	93.75
Θ	0	N/A	3
Mean σ	–	–	2.83
Max σ	–	–	8.43

σ represents the % improvement in solution fitness when soft max selection is used. Θ represents the number of additional problems solved.

Excerpt	Comments
① Table VII summarizes metadata for experiment set A using row communication, and Tables VIII and IX repeat these statistics for mesh and hybrid communication. ② In these tables, σ is the percentage improvement of the soft-max variant when compared to the solution generated by the baseline, and θ is the number of additional problems that each algorithm could solve (i.e., the number unsolvable by the baseline but solvable by the algorithm in question). ③ In calculating the percentage of problems solved, the number of problems was taken as 32, as 4 problems could not be solved by any method in any of the tests. ④ The data are also depicted as a bar chart in Fig. 4 for ease of comparison. ⑤ Note that if the sum of the percentages of best solutions is greater than 100% it is because two algorithms generated the same best solution.	

(Whitbrook, A., Meng, Q. & Chuang, P. 2018. Reliable, distributed scheduling and rescheduling for time-critical, multiagent systems. *IEEE Transactions on Automation Science and Engineering*, 15(2): 732–747.)

III. Fill the following gaps of the excerpts with appropriate words provided in the boxes below.

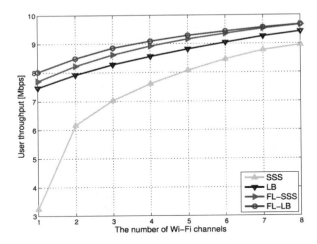

Fig. 11. User's throughput versus the number of Wi-Fi channels ($N_u = 60$).

| increases | reduced | smaller | approaches |
| decreases | compromised | affected | decreases |

Excerpt 1

As shown in Fig. 11, in general, the users' throughput _____ when the number of Wi-Fi channels is reduced. Among all the methods, the performance of the SSS _____ the most significantly. This is because the SSS assigns users to Wi-Fi regardless of its capacity and availability. Thus, when the Wi-Fi capacity is _____, the performance of those Wi-Fi users is severely _____. Unlike the SSS, the other methods have the ability to balance the loads between Li-Fi and Wi-Fi, and thus are less _____ by a reduced number of Wi-Fi channels. In addition, as the number of Wi-Fi channels _____, the performance of the FL-SSS gradually _____ that of the FL-LB. The reason for this trend is that when more users are migrated to Wi-Fi, the gap between using the LB and SSS in Li-Fi becomes _____.

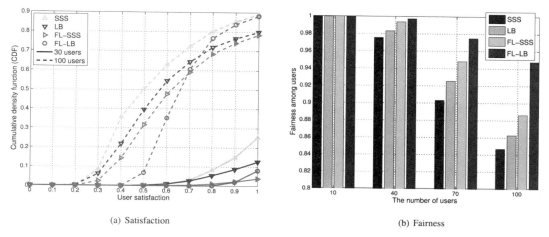

Fig. 9. System performance versus the number of users ($\bar{R} = 10$ Mbps).

| decreasing | increase | slower | increased to |
| achieves | cross point | decreases | improve |

Excerpt 2

Fig. 9 presents the users' satisfaction and fairness of various methods when the average required data rate is 10 Mbps. As shown in Fig. 9(a), the proposed method can significantly _____ the users' satisfaction over the SSS and LB, especially for a large number of users. When 30 users are present, using the SSS can meet the data requirements for only 74.6% of the users. This value is _____ 87.4% by employing the LB instead of the SSS. When using the FL-SSS and FL-LB, the proportion of satisfied users is 96.1% and 91.9%, respectively. Note that there is a _____ between the curves of the FL-SSS and FL-LB. This is because using the LB in the proposed method can _____ the performance of deeply-unsatisfied users, by _____ the number of satisfied users. In Fig. 9(b), the fairness among users is shown for different numbers of users. Two outcomes are observed: i) the fairness of all methods equals 1 given a small number of users; ii) as the number of users increases, the fairness _____ for all methods, but the fairness of the FL-LB decreases much _____ than that of the other methods. At _____ the fairness of the FL-LB _____ 0.95, while the remaining methods have a fairness below 0.9.

(Wu, X., Safari, M., & Haas, H. 2017. Access point selection for hybrid Li-Fi and Wi-Fi networks. *IEEE Transactions on Communications*, 65(12): 5375–5385.)

Chapter 5
Discussing Findings

5.1 Lead-in

Before commencing writing the Discussion section, one should consider the following questions:

1. What did you expect to find?

2. What is the basis of your assumptions?

3. What have you actually found?

4. Do your results conform to your expectations? If yes, how? If no, why?

5. How would you compare your results with the previous research?

6. How would you explain the unexpected results?

7. Is there any limitation of your research?

8. How would you further improve the research?

Unlike the Results section, which objectively reports the information you get after doing an experiment or conducting a research procedure, the Discussion section probes into the results to explain what these results indicate and their relation with previous research. For novice researchers, the Discussion section may be the most difficult section, as it requires the authors to be able to evaluate the results with accurate judgements and to put forward arguments based on the knowledge of extensive reading and discussion.

Adjusted from Glasman-Deal (2009), Swales (1990), Kanoksilapatham (2015) and consolidated by the corpus, here are some basic moves and steps that can help us in composing a well arguable discussion.

- **Move 1: Revisiting previous sections (summarizing/revisiting general or key results)**

    Step 1 Revisiting the introduction

    Step 2 Revisiting the methodology

    Step 3 Revisiting the results

- **Move 2: Consolidating results**

Chapter 5
Discussing Findings

Step 1 Reporting results

Step 2 Comparing results

Step 3 Evaluating results

- **Move 3: Stating limitations and future research**

5.2 Revisiting Previous Sections

To begin the Discussion, you can review what has been stated in the previous sections as a reminder to the reader. You can start by reviewing the Introduction, the Method or the Results. It depends on which part of the research you think is the most important for the Discussion.

5.2.1 Revisiting the Introduction

You can introduce the Discussion by reviewing the main moves in the Introduction, the background of your research, the existing research gap and the purpose of your research.

Excerpt	Comment
① Deep learning models have often achieved increasing success due to the availability of massive datasets and expanding model depth and parameterisation. ② However, in practice factors like memory and computational time during training and testing are important factors to consider when choosing a model from a large bank of models. ③ Training time becomes an important consideration particularly when the performance gain is not commensurate with increased training time as shown in our experiments. ④ Test time memory and computational load are important to deploy models on specialised embedded devices, for example, in AR applications. ⑤ From an overall efficiency viewpoint, we feel less attention has been paid to smaller and more memory, time efficient models for real-time applications such as road scene understanding and AR. ⑥ This was the primary motivation behind the proposal of SegNet, which is significantly smaller and faster than other competing architectures, but which we have shown to be efficient for tasks such as road scene understanding.	The authors revisit the Introduction of the paper. They begin by introducing the background of the research in Sentence ①. They focus on the important factors to consider in experiment and application in the next three sentences. Then, in Sentence ⑤ they point out the research gap that needs to be addressed. The last sentence in the first paragraph summarizes the previous few sentences as a reminder of the motivation of the model and describes its application.

(Badrinarayanan, V., Kendall, A. & Cipolla, R. 2017. SegNet: A deep convolutional encoder-decoder architecture for image segmentation. *IEEE Transactions on Pattern Analysis and Machine Intelligence*, *39*(12): 2481–2495.)

5.2.2 Revisiting the Methodology

If the novelty of your research lies most in your method, you can also begin your Discussion section by reminding your readers of the purpose of your research and how you have achieved it.

Excerpt	Comment
① In this paper we have discussed the principles of wireless access for Ultra-Reliable Low-Latency Communication (URLLC). ② We have used a communication-theoretic framework to provide discussion on the fundamental tradeoffs. ③ This was followed by elaboration on the important elements in access protocols. ④ Two specific technologies were considered in the context of ultra-reliable communication, massive MIMO and multi-connectivity (interface diversity). ⑤ We have also touched upon the important question about the proper statistical methodology for designing and assessing ultra-reliable communication. ⑥ However, there are also important challenges that were not treated in the paper and out of them we would like to single out the problem of design of short-length codes for URLLC, a topic treated in [83], [84]. Here we reiterate the role of Machine Learning (ML) techniques in measuring and ensuring ultra-reliability. The knowledge of the environment in which ultra-reliable connectivity takes place is crucial for guaranteeing high levels of reliability, but also for applying methods to achieve this reliability. As the simplest example, knowing the coherence bandwidth in a given Industry 4.0 setting will lead to a proper selection of the allocated frequency resources. Getting knowledge about the environment requires data-driven technique and ML methods, while it introduces training cost. We believe that one of the main next frontiers in URLLC is proper formulation of the reliability challenge as well as methods to solve it based on ML techniques. Finally, as an important next step, the community needs to address the issue of coupling high reliability with low latency, as it is done in the context of 5G. Relaxing the latency requirements towards a long term, e.g., beyond 10 or 50 ms, opens the design space for solutions that have good system level characteristics, such as coexistence with the other 5G services, or exhibit a higher energy efficiency. It should also be noted	In Sentence ①, the authors restate the main purpose of the research as an overall review of the article. In Sentence ②, the authors review the framework used in the research, and explain the important elements in access protocols in Sentences ③ and then list the technologies used in Sentence ④. Sentence ⑤ states the methodology used in the research. Then the authors describe the limitations of the current research. The second paragraph of the Discussion elaborates the methodology with details about the parameters by giving a simple example. And the authors show the contribution of the research.

Chapter 5
Discussing Findings

(Continued)

Excerpt	Comment
that the latency requirements on the wireless link can be reduced by adopting a holistic system design. For example, requiring 1 ms from the wireless link, while allowing source compression procedures that introduce much larger delay, is certainly not the optimal approach. Hence, one is tempted to define new research problems related to joint source-channel coding and protocol design that are suited to meet end-to-end latency and reliability requirements.	In the last paragraph, the authors suggest the specific areas or research questions that can be addressed in future work.

(Popovski, P., Stefanović, Č., Nielsen, J. J., De Carvalho, E., Angjelichinoski, M., Trillingsgaard, K. F. & Bana, A. S. 2019. Wireless access in ultra-reliable low-latency communication (URLLC). *IEEE Transactions on Communications*, *67*(8): 5783–5801.)

5.2.3 Revisiting the Results

You can also begin your Discussion by reviewing the main findings of the Results section.

Excerpt	Comment
① We have shown that temporal fluorescence data can be used to precisely localize a set of point fluorescent emitters in a homogeneous heavily scattering environment. ② For an inhomogeneous domain, the background scattering parameters could be estimated from prior measurements using established reconstruction methods. ③ If substantial background signal is present (from tissue autofluorescence, for example), it could be subtracted from the measured data in a calibration step, or incorporated into the forward model, (11), through the addition of a background source term. ④ We assumed a fixed and known fluorescence lifetime for all reporters. ⑤ While this may be appropriate for some applications, if there should be variations in lifetime because of the local (chemical) environment, lifetime could be estimated along with position, in a revised interpretation of the cost function in (16).	The authors begin the Discussion section by summarizing the main finding of the research in Sentence ①. And they then add more details in Sentences ② to ⑤.

95

(Continued)

Excerpt	Comment
⑥ We have analyzed several requirements of being able to successfully detect and localize fluorescent emitters. ⑦ Appendix B develops a method for detecting individual emitters during a temporal scan, and its success depends on the yield, η, as well as the SNR. ⑧ For this detection method to work, fluorescent emissions must be separated in time by at least the window duration, w, a requirement that is explored in Section III-C. ⑨ It is important to note that this requirement for a separation in time places an implicit constraint on the sampling period. ⑩ Namely, the sampling period must be short enough so as to not hide this existing temporal separation. ⑪ Furthermore, for such emitters to be fully distinguishable, their spatial locations must be separated by at least the localization uncertainty described in Section IV-A, otherwise, while they may be detectable, they will be mistaken for the same emitter. ⑫ If all of these conditions are met, then all fluorescent emitters will be detectable and distinguishable from one another. ⑬ In the case where the same emitter is localized several times because its light is emitted at multiple delays separated by at least the window length, the emitter could be identified through calculation of its localization uncertainty.	In the second paragraph, the authors briefly summarizes the methodology part in Sentence ⑥, and provides details about how they get the results in Sentences ⑦ and ⑧. The rest of the sentences discuss how their method and results would be applicable.

(Bentz, B. Z., Lin, D., Patel, J. A. & Webb, K. J. 2019. Multiresolution localization with temporal scanning for super-resolution diffuse optical imaging of fluorescence. *IEEE Transactions on Image Processing*, 29: 830–842.)

The following sentence structures can be used to revisit the previous sections.

* *We first evaluate the accuracy of the proposed... We then study the effects of...on...as well as...efficiency to...*
* *Before concluding, we wish to draw some reflections out from the above results and from our experience of managing..., and to offer some recommendations for future...*
* *Before concluding our paper, we discuss challenges for future work that need to be overcome in order to make...methods for...a practical component of operations and management of...*
* *We proposed a reasonable solution for... For..., our...calculate...; therefore, ... This calculation increases linearly according to... Therefore...*

> * *We have shed some light on...: (1) a...model with...and (2) ... We focused on...: ...for... and...for... More...methods are conceivable to account for..., for instance. However, even with our current set-up, ...can...*
> * *We have introduced a framework for..., both across...and across..., that works across...and requires fewer...than other state-of-the-art methods for..., representing an effective combination of...and...*
> * *We have exploited... In our proposed scheme, we have selected..., therefore, the algorithm we employ can be considered as a...one. To give further insight into..., we show...*
> * *In order to gain further insights into..., we use the theory of...to help us. We start with a brief introduction to...and a review of pertinent results. In this work, we assume that... We now describe...*
> * *We proposed a reasonable solution for...(summary of key results). An important assumption of...is that... If..., ...does not work. Thus, we assume... Therefore...*
> * *The framework discussed in this paper has already been successfully applied to a number of different use cases in the context of... For instance, ... In this section, we describe...*
> * *We use the results derived for...to evaluate... The main objective is to demonstrate how... The analytical results here are supported further by the numerical results in section x.*
> * *In this paper, we have discussed the principles of... We have used a...framework to provide discussion on... This was followed by elaboration on... Two specific technologies were considered in the context of... We have also touched upon the important question about...methodology for... Here we reiterate the role of...in...*
> * *...enable... Adopting this paradigm proposed by..., we have shown...*

5.3 Consolidating Results

This is the main part of the discussion, which reveals the authors' perception of the results. It is also the most difficult part, as the perspective of the discussion of results can reflect the authors' understanding of the field; i.e., whether they are able to interpret the results from an appropriate point of view, whether they can compare or contrast their results with the most relevant ones in literature, and what conclusions they can draw from the explanation and comparison.

5.3.1 Reporting Results

The authors should be able to make a claim about the most important findings and develop their argumentation with the detailed explanations and examples.

Excerpt	Comment
① The tradeoff between solution quality and run-time efficiency is an important factor in both sets of experiments, and a key consideration is that the soft-max variant is not as efficient as the baseline in terms of execution time. ② This matters more for shorter mission times such as those considered in experiment set A, where the maximum mission time is 2000 s (about half an hour), and mean rescue times are at about 280 s (about four and a half minutes). ③ In these problems, any saving in mean rescue time offered by the soft-max variant is counter-balanced by run-time losses. ④ For example, if there is a 4% saving in mean rescue time, this equates to about 11 s for each task. If there are 28 tasks, the total saving is 308 s or about 5 min. ⑤ However, if the search algorithm takes 5 min to run, then any gain is eliminated. ⑥ For smaller time scale problems, this means that it is important to terminate the algorithm execution early or limit the search space some other way as m increases, even if this means missing fitter solutions. ⑦ However, for more realistic larger-scale problems, for example, problems with a maximum mission time in terms of days and mean rescue start times in terms of hours, the algorithm's initial run-time efficiency is not as important and thus has much less impact on overall mean rescue time. ⑧ In these cases, it would be possible to examine a wider range of the spectrum of possible τ values to be certain of finding the optimal or near-optimal solution without compromising the effectiveness or efficiency of the mission. ⑨ In addition, a possible application is to reserve use of the soft-max module only for cases where baseline PI fails to solve. ⑩ These experiments have illustrated that PI is much more effective than CBBA in solving both lower dimensioned problems with tight constraints and higher dimensioned problems with more relaxed constraints. ⑪ They have also demonstrated that PI's performance can be enhanced easily by making some adjustments to the action-selection mechanism within the task removal and task inclusion phases of the algorithm.	In Sentence ①, the authors point out an important factor that can influence the results. Then, they explain the effect of the factor in different situations in detail from Sentence ③ to Sentence ⑦, in which specific examples and results are given to illustrate the authors' claim in Sentence ①. In Sentences ⑧ and ⑨, after presenting the key findings of different problems, the authors give suggestions about how to get the best solution and possible application of the model. In the last paragraph, the authors claim the values of the results.

(Whitbrook, A., Meng, Q. & Chung, P. W. 2017. Reliable, distributed scheduling and rescheduling for time-critical, multiagent systems. *IEEE Transactions on Automation Science and Engineering*, 15(2): 732–747.)

Chapter 5
Discussing Findings

The Discussion section is also heavily embedded with figures and tables, according to which, the interpretation of results can follow a structure like this:

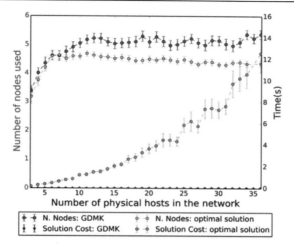

Fig. 5. Varying the number of physical hosts from 1 to 36.

Excerpt	Comment
① The experiment in Fig. 5 shows how the underlying topologies impact both the optimal solution (OCNSD) and the proposed heuristic (GDMK). ② We vary the number of physical hosts belonging to the physical layer in our proposed architecture while fixing the number of network slices, SFCs, NFs. ③ Concerning the optimal solution, the first observation that we can draw from this figure is that the number of used nodes, represented by the pentagon shape, stagnates in 5, even when increasing the number of physical hosts 5 fold. ④ Moreover, we clearly observe the exponential behavior of the computational time, expressed by the hexagon shape, which allow us to conclude that when we increase the number of underlying nodes, the number of links between those nodes increases due to the higher density of nodes in our network which will raise the probability of deployment of the network slices causing by the same time the exponential growth in the computational time (optimal solution search always best options). ⑤ For the heuristic solution, the same stagnation in terms of the number of used nodes, represented by the circle shape, is observed with a higher number of the used nodes (6 for the heuristic instead of 5 for the optimal solution). ⑥ However, the computational time for the heuristic solution is linear and has the following linear regression samples 0.0096 and 0.00099, as α and β, respectively.	Sentence ① locates the description to Fig.5 and summarizes the main information of the figure. Sentence ② explains how the authors get the results in this figure. Sentence ③ states the first observation from the figure. Sentence ④ describes another observation, followed by the interpretation of the results. Sentence ⑤ states another observation with supportive details.

(Addad, R. A., Bagaa, M., Taleb, T., Dutra, D. L. C. & Flinck, H. 2019. Optimization model for cross-domain network slices in 5G networks. *IEEE Transactions on Mobile Computing, 19*(5): 1156–1169.)

More sentence patterns to report the results are as follows.

> * *The...plays a key role in... When..., ...be...*
> * *Through our discussions and experimental evaluation, we have demonstrated the effectiveness of...for...*
> * *Adopting this paradigm proposed by [reference], we have shown the existence of a...systems that allows us to ...*
> * *To apply these theorems, we first make the following observation about...*
> * *To illustrate the effect of...on..., Fig. x shows...on...*
> * *In all three cases shown in Fig. x, the x for each deployment decreases rapidly with increasing...*
> * *It is clear from our experiments and other independent benchmarks [references] that...*
> * *The heuristic explanation for the...model lies in the fact that... There are multiple possible...that can lead to the same set of measurement data. For example, assume...is... This would result in..., so... would be impossible.*
> * *There are three major types of...encountered in... The first two deal with..., and the third deals with...*
> * *In this section, we discuss the...technique proposed to solve the...problem. Since...for the...introduced in Problem x cannot be easily obtained, a systematic method for..., which..., leading to...is provided. The method requires..., which... It is shown that the...methodology, which leads to approximate solutions of...in Problem x, yields a solution to...*

5.3.2 Comparing Results

To consolidate your results, sometimes you need to compare them with other research.

Excerpt	Comment
① The effectiveness of the proposed method will now be verified by means of a simulation example. ② In particular, we will conduct comparison of the proposed model reference scheme using reaching law (12) with the one introduced in [33] where Gao's classic reaching law is used instead. ③ It will be shown that the new strategy can successfully be applied to a plant with unmatched disturbance and that it ensures better system robustness than its relative degree one equivalent.	Sentence ① states the purpose of the Discussion. Sentence ② explains how the effectiveness of the method will be evaluated. Sentence ③ presents the result of the comparison.

(Latosiński, P. & Bartoszewicz, A. 2020. Model reference DSMC with a relative degree two switching variable. *IEEE Transactions on Automatic Control, 66*(4): 1749–1755.)

Chapter 5
Discussing Findings

Excerpt	Comment
① We compare our method to Matching Pursuit, and extensions to that method do exist, one being Orthogonal Matching Pursuit (OMP). ② Rather than calculating basis function weights once, OMP recalculates them upon every iteration, thereby mitigating error accumulation. ③ Taking inspiration from OMP, we could reduce potential error accumulation in the estimated ηk by recalculating all of their values upon each successive detection of a fluorescent emitter. ④ Other super-resolution methods have been developed for improving the spatial resolution beyond the diffraction limit in microscopy. ⑤ Fundamentally, imaging methods can surpass resolution limits with the addition of prior information to compensate for the information that is lost due to attenuation or randomization of the signal. ⑥ For example, structured illumination microscopy (SIM) breaks the resolution limit through spatial modulation of the excitation light, and can be further improved by leveraging the nonlinear dependence of the fluorescent emission rate in the saturation regime. ⑦ Stimulated emission depletion (STED) forms a smaller effective point spread function (PSF) by saturating fluorophores at the periphery of the focal point. ⑧ Other techniques such as photo activated localization microscopy (PALM), fluorescence PALM (fPALM), and stochastic optical reconstruction microscopy (STORM) are able to localize switchable fluorescent molecules by distinguishing the emission between their fluorescent and non-fluorescent states. ⑨ These are all super-resolution methods that achieve position information beyond that directly represented by the point spread function. ⑩ The shared use of temporal switching of fluorescence states influorescent molecules makes our method analogous to PALM, fPALM, and STORM. ⑪ However, our incorporation of a forward model, such as the coupled diffusion model for scattered light we use here, allows imaging through scatter. ⑫ Moreover, our super-resolution imaging methodcan be applied to a wider variety of applications that employ forward models, such as photoacoustic tomography, electrical impedance tomography, and microwave imaging.	The authors compare their method to another one, and point out the mechanism of the compared method in the first two sentences. Then, they explain what they can benefit from the comparison. They describe other relevant methods with examples in Sentence ④ to Sentence ⑧. Sentence ⑨ summarizes the previously mentioned methods, and Sentence ⑩ relates the methods to the authors' method. In the following two sentences, the advantages of the authors' method are highlighted through comparison.

(Bentz, B. Z., Lin, D., Patel, J. A. & Webb, K. J. 2019. Multiresolution localization with temporal scanning for super-resolution diffuse optical imaging of fluorescence. *IEEE Transactions on Image Processing, 29*: 830–842.)

To indicate the comparison, you can use the following sentence patterns.

* *We compare our method to..., and extensions to that method do exist, one being...*
* *Results of this comparison are illustrated by the following three figures depicting..., ...and...*
* *Additionally, a numerical comparison of...for both strategies has been conducted using two criteria:...and...*
* *An interesting point of comparison is provided by similar challenges run via... such as...*
* *To give further insight into..., we show the comparison of...and the proposed...in Fig. x.*
* *The effectiveness of the proposed method will now be verified by means of a...example. In particular, we will conduct comparison of the proposed... scheme using...with the one introduced in [reference] where...is used instead.*
* *A comparison with state-of-the-art...algorithms has shown that, in most of the considered situations, ...outperforms its competitors.*
* *These...are examined and compared with...in this database. A...algorithm is implemented wherein...is compared with...in the database.*
* *The results of extensive testing of the...algorithm have validated its architecture and demonstrated benefits compared with...*
* *Comparing this scheme with the...scheme, it is clear that the...scheme is easier to implement.*
* *Previous work in...focuses on...such that..., here referred to as... In contrast, our method treats...as...whose...*
* *First, this paper focuses on creating a...to define...rules of the...system. The...are defined creating... In contrast, the work in [reference] creates a different...for...*
* *To the best of our knowledge, the only previous work related to our solution is [reference], which describes a...framework called... However, there are several differences between the work in [reference] and ours. First, ...*
* *The effectiveness of the proposed method will now be verified by means of... In particular, we will conduct comparison of the proposed model reference scheme using...with the one introduced in... It will be shown that...*
* *Although the various...paradigms may be...from different aspects of the problem, they can be decomposed into the x components depicted in Fig. x. We discuss them one by one.*
* *The usual approach to show the usefulness of a new...technique is to apply it to a number of different problems and to compare its performance with that of already available techniques. In the case of..., this type of research initially consisted of testing the algorithms on the...*

To show the advantages of your research, you can use sentence patterns like the following.

* *We have shed some light on... We focused on... More expressive representations and...methods are conceivable to account for..., for instance. However, ...*
* *The...framework is not shown in the figure since it is not yet... As the figure shows, our approach brought better results than the existing ones.*
* *More recently, a...designed for the challenging...was shown to be competitive with state-of-the-art...algorithms [references], while at the same time offering better...*
* *This method works better than...both in...case and after...period.*
* *There are also instances in which...that do actually contribute to..., and we have shown that...is robust to...*
* *Previous work has shown that...is useful in... [references]. The...is a close approximation to...that results from...as a...process, a common assumption for...*
* *Although the various...paradigms may be motivated and derived from different aspects of the problem, they can be decomposed into the five components depicted in Fig. x. We discuss them one by one.*
* *...have often achieved increasing success due to... However, in practice factors like...and...are important factors to consider when...// ...becomes an important consideration particularly when...as shown in our experiments. From an overall viewpoint, we feel less attention has been paid to..., ...and... This was the primary motivation behind the proposal of..., which is significantly...than other competing architectures, but which we have shown to be efficient for tasks such as...*
* *Comparing the proposed...approach to...suggests that... In order to evaluate this observation in a...context, the architecture of the...was modified by... This amounts to... When tested on..., the... model achieves..., whereas the original architecture achieves... The same experiment on...shows a similar result as the...model obtains..., compared to... obtained by the...model. To test whether...leads to..., the models trained on...are additionally tested on... The...model achieves a...of..., and is outperformed by the original architecture with a...of... The differences are rather small, but it shows that the deeper and more complex model does lead to a more accurate prediction. However, when...is important, small improvements might not justify the...increase in the number of parameters.*

5.3.3 Evaluating Results

The evaluation of the results usually takes a few sentences to show the contribution or significance of the research.

* *This...approach has some advantages.*
* *One of the key aspects of the proposed framework is..., which has a strong impact on...*
* *Our approach achieves a good performance in terms of...// ...achieves good...results, with significantly more/less...than... (see Fig. x for example).*
* *As mentioned in Sections II and III, one important property of the method is that, ... In this work, the method has been implemented using..., leading to an average processing time of...per...*
* *This figure illustrates the importance of studying...for..., as it helps..., which could be implemented in practice.*
* *Even though the proposed methods outperform comparable methods, is still far from being satisfactory. Despite..., ... Thus, ...has the same shortcomings as...*
* *The remarkably better performance of...implies the importance of... Since..., considering...leads to...while other...models are focused only on...such as...*
* *This is a significant finding, which opens a new area of..., in which...can be traded off to achieve better performance. For instance, ...*
* *For the analysis of the results, we will first apply a...test [reference] to determine if there are significant differences between...and...*
* *The obtained results were good for scenarios where...*
* *The...results on...are reported in the right half of Table x. For these..., the...hypothesis is very clearly rejected as there is a growing performance gap between...and our... The...generalizes better to..., even performing close to optimal up to... The further..., the larger is the performance gap between...and... Although both...perform well for..., the...clearly outperforms on...*
* *The findings made based on the...results are also supported by...reported in Table x. ...results in the best overall performance in terms of...and... While providing reasonably convincing...results, ...produces only average...and even results in the lowest...among all tested models on... This result is expected and is observed regularly in the literature [reference] with... methods.// ...and...improve upon...in terms of..., but are less competitive in comparison to the top performers of this experiment.*
* *One of...benefits is...by explicitly incorporating...into planning and control.// ..., however, does not take...into account. Instead, ... On the other hand, ...*

5.4 Stating Limitations and Future Research

In the end of a research article, you usually need to state the limitations of your research and then propose directions for future improvement and research accordingly. If some of the results are out of your expectation, you can also provide possible explanations so as to make improvement in future.

Chapter 5
Discussing Findings

Excerpt	Comment
Even though the results obtained are more than encouraging with respect to the applicability and efficacy of DL for affective modeling, there are a number of research directions that should be considered in future research. While the Maze-Ball game dataset includes key components for affective modeling and is representative of a typical affective modeling scenario, our PDLv approach needs to be tested on diverse datasets. The reduced size of the dataset limited the number of features that could be learned. Currently, deep architectures are widely used to extract thousands of features from large datasets, which yields models that outperform other state-of-the-art classification or regression methods (e.g., [27]). We expect that the application of DL to model affect in large physiological datasets would show larger improvements with respect to statistical features and provide new insights on the relationship between physiology and affect. Moreover, to be able to demonstrate robustness of the algorithm, more and dissimilar modalities of user input need to be considered, and different domains (beyond games) need to be explored. To that end, different approaches to multimodal fusion in conjunction with DL need to be investigated. The accuracies obtained across different affective states and modalities of user input, however, already provide sufficient evidence that the method would generalize well in dissimilar domains and modalities.	The authors acknowledge the encouraging results obtained in the previous section, and then point out the future research directions. Then, they elaborate on the points that could be further developed in future.
The paper did not provide a thorough analysis of the impact of feature selection to the efficiency of DL as the focus was put on feature extraction. To that end, more feature selection methods will need to be investigated and compared to SFS. While ad-hoc feature performances might be improved with more advanced FS methods, such as genetic search based FS, the obtained results already show that DL matches and even beats a rather effective and popular FS mechanism without the use of feature selection in several experiments. Although in this paper we have compared DL to a complete and representative set of ad-hoc features, a wider set of features could be explored in future work. For instance, heart rate variability features derived from the Fourier transformation of BVP (see [33]) could be included in the comparison. However, it is expected that CNNs would be able to extract relevant frequency-based features as their successful application in other domains already demonstrates (e.g., music sample classification). Furthermore, other automatic feature extraction methods, such as principal component analysis, which is common in domains, such as	In the second paragraph, the authors first explain why the paper did not provide a thorough analysis, and then point out how some features of their model could be improved in future.

(Continued)

Excerpt	Comment
image classification, will be explored for psycho-physiological modeling and compared to DL in this domain. Despite the good results reported in this paper on the skin conductance and blood volume pulse signals, we expect that certain well-designed ad-hoc features can still outperform automatically learned features. Within playing behavioral attributes, for example, the final score of a game—which is highly correlated to reported fun in games—may not be captured by convolutional networks, which tend to find patterns that are invariant with respect to the position in the signal. Such an ad-hoc feature, however, may carry information of high predictive power for particular affective states. We argue that DL is expected to be of limited use in low resolution signals (e.g., player score over time) which could generate well-defined feature spaces for affective modeling. An advantage of ad-hoc extracted statistical features resides in the simplicity to interpret the physical properties of the signal as they are usually based on simple statistical metrics. Therefore, prediction models trained on statistical features can be analyzed with low effort providing insights in affective phenomena. Artificial neural networks have traditionally been considered as black boxes that oppose their high prediction power to a more difficult interpretation of what has been learned by the model. We have shown, however, that appropriate visualization tools can ease the interpretation of neural-network based features. Moreover, learned features derived from DL architectures may define data-based extracted patterns, which could lead to the advancement of our understanding of emotion manifestations via physiology (and beyond). Finally, while DL can automatically provide a more complete and appropriate set of features when compared to adhoc feature extraction, parameter tuning is a necessary phase in (and a limitation of) the training process. This paper introduced a number of CNN topologies that performed well on the SC and BVP signals while empirical results showed that, in general, the performance of the CNN topologies is not affected significantly by parameter tuning. Future work, however, would aim to further test the sensitivity of CNN topologies and parameter sets as well as the generality of the extracted features across physiological datasets, reducing the experimentation effort required for future applications of DL to psychophysiology.	The authors make another claim about future research in detail. By showing the advantage of the current research, the authors make suggestions for future research. Finally, the authors summarize the main contributions and results of the research and propose future research direction.

(Martinez, H. P., Bengio, Y. & Yannakakis, G. N. 2013. Learning deep physiological models of affect. *IEEE Computational Intelligence Magazine*, 8(2): 20–33.)

Chapter 5
Discussing Findings

You can use the following sentences to state limitations of the current research.

* *Though the proposed...method appears to work well across datasets, it has some undesirable features. One such characteristic of the proposed...method is...*
* *We think the...has still limitations. The...can deal with the difference of...between...and... However, the...cannot cope with...because... How to take newness of records into account is left to the future work.*
* *Our...also has difficulty on..., that is, ... When using..., we have to... Although this process can be done in..., the calculation cost is high especially when ...*
* *A second problematic result of using...is..., as...*
* *An important choice we had to make when...was... Many of these architectures have used...to..., but this makes it difficult to... Instead, we chose to... However, we note that this approach cannot...in achieving a particular result. This is mainly due to the fact that... Acknowledging these shortcomings, our hope is that this...analysis complements other benchmarks [references] and reveals...in different well known architectures.*

You can use the following sentences to indicate possible future research directions.

* *Even though the results obtained are more than encouraging with respect to..., there are a number of research directions that should be considered in future research.*
* *Before concluding our paper, we discuss challenges for future work that need to be overcome in order to...*
* *Further work may determine an appropriate criterion to... For practical application, however, we found no obvious trend as to... Our suggestion with this method would be to...*
* *One possible future direction is to specify our priors as samples from a...process and attempt to take advantage of any...because...[reference], as has been shown to be effective in...[reference]. It is also interesting to note that..., which suggests that... Further work with this approach in...should prove to be very interesting.*
* *For the future, we would like to exploit our understanding of...architectures gathered from our analysis to design more efficient architectures for real-time applications.*
* *Further work with this approach in...or...should prove to be very interesting.*
* *It is also instructive to look at the correlation between...and... It allows us to study...using...*
* *For the future, we would like to exploit our understanding of...to design more efficient architectures for real-time applications. We are also interested in...*
* *Although there are studies analyzing the influence of...on...systematically [references], we are not aware of any unified framework to study... However, albeit being a promising*

> *framework, a fair comparison, e.g., to the...[reference] would require an analysis of...*
> * *Hence, while the proposed...offers..., the difference here is less significant for a larger volume. However, our framework could be further improved in several ways. An option would be to... The proposed framework could also be combined with the...approach proposed in [reference] to perform..., which demonstrates... We expect that...would further improve the performance of the method while...as demonstrated in Section x. These extensions are to be addressed in future works.*

5.5 Language Focus

5.5.1 Moderating a Claim

While discussing the results, the authors' attitude is often reflected by the claim. In order to appropriately show the strength of the claim, some rhetoric can be used.

1) Polarity and Modality

One of the most effective ways to moderate a claim is to add different degrees of probability and usuality by using modal verbs, such as *will, can, may*; or adverbs, such as *always, usually, probably*, or both together, such as *will probably, may possibly* (Halliday & Matthiessen, 2014). For detailed explanation, please see Section 2.3.5. Here are some examples with modal verbs or adverbs or both to show moderated claims.

> * *The...<u>can be</u> envisioned as a...system, where each layer provides different types of... for..., ...and...*
> * *Imaging <u>can be expected to be</u> more accurate in areas where...than in areas where ...*
> * *Since...are ubiquitous in systems and control, we expect that our approach <u>could lead to</u>...solutions to many other control problems.*
> * *...<u>may also prove</u> a useful addition to make...for general purposes as in... [reference].*
> * *Doing...and using...<u>may be beneficial to</u> improve...accuracy.*
> * *... <u>would likely be</u> coupled with..., which could be an additional driving force for...*
> * *When..., ...<u>are likely to fail</u> to...*
> * *While there is no clear rule as to when it <u>might be necessary</u>, we can easily see <u>a possible explanation for</u> this problem when considering the...method itself.*

2) Distance

Distance means "removing yourself from a strong and possibly unjustified claim" (Swales & Feak, 2012, p. 160). For example:

* ...<u>may seem</u> too trivial, yet the advantage of a fixed model is that...
* ...<u>tend to</u> reduce...and hence...
* Though the proposed...method <u>appears to work well</u> across datasets, it has some undesirable features.
* A comparison with state-of-the-art routing algorithms has shown that, <u>in most of the considered situations</u>, ...outperforms its competitors.
* Even if this system is a simple application of the..., it still involves a number of different devices and...technologies, thus being representative of <u>most of</u> the critical issues that need to be taken care of when designing...
* Common to <u>many of</u> these applications is that the best performing...algorithms make intensive use of...
* In...problems, <u>some</u> variables have a stochastic nature.
* The algorithm was able <u>to solve some problems</u> that failed using...
* <u>Apart from</u> the...problems, for which the main focus was put on..., the... problem was the first...problem tackled by...algorithms.

3) Cause and Effect

While discussing findings, cause-and-effect statements are often used. These statements can take different forms, such as adverbial phrases, verbs, or conjunctions. It is found in the corpus that conjunctions are the most used and verbs are the least.

* <u>As a result,</u> even though the...technology provides..., ...are not part of the...network and have to rely their...on...
* <u>As a result of this study on</u> the current state of...solution for..., several key trends have been identified that could shape the future of...solutions.
* <u>As a result,</u> our method is complementary to...methods.
* However, the...cannot cope with...<u>because</u>...
* As..., ...outperforms...<u>because</u>..., and...
* Fundamentally, ...methods can surpass resolution limits with the addition of prior information to compensate for...that is...<u>due to</u>...
* However, <u>due to</u>...and..., their...are different.
* Furthermore, when..., the...information is more concentrated on... <u>This is due to</u> the...function that is...
* In fact, a significant change of..., whether...or..., can <u>lead to</u>...that would not normally happen for...with...
* ...features derived from...architectures may define...patterns, which could <u>lead to</u> the advancement of our understanding of...via...

* *The separate implementation of...and...<u>results in</u>..., due to...devices required in..., as well as...*
* *However, in practice we found... The other option is to use...method, which <u>results in</u> a...that...*
* *The...is a close approximation to...that <u>results from</u>..., a common assumption for...*

 **Exercises**

I. Please try to use some modifications, such as *could, can, may, might, should, probably, possible, sometimes, seem, appear, some, etc.*, to soften the claims.

1. Taking inspiration from OMP, we reduce potential error accumulation in the estimated nk by recalculating all of their values upon each successive detection of a fluorescent emitter.

2. Our super-resolution imaging method is applied to a wider variety of applications that employ forward models.

3. Each node publishes its own features and data by running a CoAP server, though this feature is not yet implemented in the testbed.

4. The proxy logic is extended to better support monitoring applications and limit the amount of traffic injected into the IoT peripheral network.

5. Examining the readings of the other sensors in the same time interval, we note a sharp decrease of light intensity and temperature, and an increase in humidity.

6. Several applications with different performance requirements require access to the same piece of information at the same time.

7. The reduction in resource requirements allow sensing and connectivity to migrate into very low-power wearable devices, reducing the cost and complexity of contemporary health-aware clothing.

8. When the target appearance changes gradually the prediction succeeds.

9. All the methods presented here perform better if prior knowledge had been incorporated into choosing the feature space.

10. In passive (data-only) systems, sensors fail, connections drop, or a proxy's model is proven inaccurate or incomplete.

II. Please try to rewrite the following statements by using appropriate verbs, adverbs or conjunctions to indicate the cause-and-effect relations.

1. The IoT devices could be part of different management domains during their lifetimes. That information would be spread among many nodes making it difficult to audit and track it.

2. Public lighting operators will be equipped with mobile devices that can locate the streetlight that requires intervention, issue actuation commands directly to the IoT node connected to the lamp, and signal the result of the intervention to the central system that can track every single lamppost. Public lighting operators optimize the maintenance plan.

3. The SPC cannot cope with the concept change within a user. The SPC does not have any mechanism to forget old records.

4. The work represents an important extension to the baseline as real missions take place in dynamically changing environments where the SA is subject to alter rapidly. Task allocation strategies must be able to adjust to new data and recompute new solutions in real time.

5. It is possible to specify a list of resources that need to be monitored. The server can autonomously update the entries in a cache related to those devices.

6. An approach based on hierarchical reinforcement learning (HRL) was chosen. It is a promising approach to expand traditional RL methods to work with more difficult and complex tasks.

Chapter 6
Writing Abstract

6.1 Lead-in

Can you categorize the following phrases into different groups? And what is your standard of categorization?

1. This paper focuses on...

2. ...has become a promising topic in...

3. This paper proposes a...scheme to...

4. We present an algorithm for...in order to...

5. This paper aims to investigate...

6. First, we determine..., and then...

7. Adopting a...method, a...is proposed to...

8. We address this issue by adopting a...approach.

9. It is shown that...

10. The computational results reveal that...

The abstract provides an overview of the article. It summarizes each section of the article and with an emphasis on main findings.

Generally, the abstract consists of four parts that are consistent with the main parts of the article: Introduction, Methods, Results and Discussion. However, the abstract usually has a certain word limit, ranging from 150 to 300 words. In this case, to present the most distinctive contribution of the article, the abstract can omit the Introduction part and combine the Methods and Results, thus leaving space for the Discussion.

The Moves in an abstract can be identified as the following.

- **Move 1: Introducing research topic**

    Step 1 Indicating the research background

    Step 2 Presenting the purpose of the research or summarizing the research

- **Move 2: Describing the research method**
- **Move 3: Summarizing the research results**
- **Move 4: Presenting the research conclusions**

6.2 Introducing Research Topic

The abstract usually begins with introducing the background of the research. It can describe the problem existing in a certain field, the significance of the current research or the purpose of the research.

6.2.1 Indicating the Research Background

In the beginning of an abstract, we can use the following sentences to indicate the research background.

* ...often present a...architecture, requiring... This leads to... Motivated by this..., in this paper we present a...scheme to provide...for...
* This paper addresses two main problems with...approaches—...and...
* Some methods developed in...make use of...// ...may also be exploited in...; this has become a research interest in recent years because of the development of...and a need for...This paper presents a...that employs...
* This paper proposes a novel approach for...
* We present a...for... This...is suitable for...applications in which...are acquired at a fast rate.
* Due to the..., the...keeps varying with time depending on...conditions. Moreover, the varying...conditions could also lead to... These factors affect...and cause... Hence, it is important to...so that...can be... However, ... is challenging as it is determined by...
* This paper describes...in...specification and the driving motivations behind its design.
* In this paper, we describe a...design that enables a higher...than the...standard.
* The...standard has been developed with the main goal of providing significantly improved...compared with its predecessors.
* ...and...are emergent signals being used in many areas, such as...and... In particular, for...applications, they allow...in which the user can... Current approaches for..., however, present many open technical challenges and... Some of the...are specific to the...and often differ from those encountered in classical...
* ...and...are an emerging technology for... This...combines...and...techniques. While a... network can improve..., it also challenges...due to...

* *Combining...and..., ...and...are recently proposed to improve... Meanwhile, ...becomes a challenging issue due to...// ...and...further complicate..., since the decision for...is non-trivial. These issues are managed separately in most conventional methods, which might cause...and... A few studies address these issues jointly for...but...*
* *...is a...solution for... Unlike conventional...systems, the...is not isotropic, meaning that... However, due to the lack of a proper model for..., many studies have assumed that... In this paper, a novel model for...based on...has been proposed.*
* *In...systems, it may not be power efficient to have...for...*
* *In recent years, in order to provide a better quality of service (QoS) to..., ... has shifted toward... However, ...is limited and it is essential to efficiently bind...with...*
* *The future...will feature... The coupling of...and...in...use cases makes...very challenging, in terms of...and of...*
* *...consists of...It is especially practical as...when...*
* *One of the main challenges in...using...is... This...also prevents...using existing techniques.*
* *...reconstructs... A crucial step in...is..., which resolves a...structure from...by...*
* *...has piqued researchers interests in...networks. // ..., in such systems is of paramount importance.*
* *Recently, many efforts have been made to develop...for..., as well as for... Because...are often not feasible, ...is strongly demanded for...*
* *It is now commonly agreed that...// ...will also have an impact on...// ...will open the door to... In this new context, how to...and how to...become fundamental problems that need to be solved.*
* *...enables... While...become widespread in the market, the...technology is yet limited in...*
* *While...and...are two closely related and fundamental tasks in..., previous methods approach them..., failing to... In view of the existing gap between... and..., we propose to solve them together using a...*
* *The continuous development and usage of...have contributed to the exponential growth of... In this context, ...plays a critical role in...such as..., ..., and... Thus, a...paradigm for...is highly desired to meet the increasing...requirements.*
* *Bridging the gap between...and...has not yet been accomplished on a large scale. // ...is a promising way to do this.*
* *...has been a promising direction in...for more than a decade since... However, ...approaches typically require..., which is a practical limitation in real systems, such as ..., where...can be impractical and time consuming.*
* *...is an emerging paradigm that provides...to..., enabling...*

6.2.2 Presenting the Purpose of the Research or Summarizing the Research

We can also present the purpose of the research or summarize the research in the beginning of an abstract, by using the following sentence structures.

* *In this paper, a...for...model with...matrices is proposed.*
* *This paper considers the problem of...in order to optimally detect...in a...system, under the assumption that...*
* *We introduce the concept of a...contraction metric, extending...to...*
* *We propose a...scheme which combines the advantages of...and...*
* *...can be defined by..., ..., and... In this work, we present a hybrid model of...combining..., ..., and...*
* *...have experienced a continuous increase in relevance for..., because of... In this work, we introduce a new...scheme that exploits a combination of the concepts of...and...to provide near-optimal performances with ...*
* *In this paper, a...for...systems is proposed where..., i.e., ...*
* *In this paper, a...strategy based on...is introduced.*
* *In this paper, we formulate a joint...and...problem in the...network, considering the evergrowing demand of...imposed by...*
* *The...offers excellent opportunities to...due to... This paper presents experimental measurements and...models for..., using...*
* *This paper aims to provide a broad perspective on..., as well as the principles used in building...*
* *In this paper, we present an algorithm for...using...*
* *In this paper we address the problem of...from...*
* *A...method is presented to determine...*
* *To..., ...are introduced into... The...and...can lead to..., as well as... Such...will affect...and consequently... Therefore, research into objective methods for...has received attention in recent years. In this paper, we proposed a... for...based on a...scheme.*
* *To stimulate research in this field we conducted a public research challenge: ...*

6.3 Describing the Research Method

Then, we need to briefly describe the research method used in the research. The following sentence structures are useful.

* *An approximation of this...based on...is proposed and the accuracy of this*

approximation is confirmed by... Moreover, the statistics of...are calculated and...is modeled as a random process. The influence of...on...has been evaluated. Finally, a...model is proposed by considering... The performance of...is assessed on...and it is shown that it is important to take...into account.

* The exhaustive search over all the possible...is relaxed to formulate a...problem. Then, the...problem is converted into a...problem which can be efficiently solved. Using the solution, the...can perform... To further improve...performance, we also develop a...that exploits...
* First, we determine the priority of different...by enforcing the analytical framework using... Using..., we then formulate a...game to initiate... Subsequently, we consider...in the...game that occurs due to...and solve the...problem by applying...
* More than...were measured across...bands to yield...
* Adopting a...approach, a...model is constructed to capture...and a...scheme based on...is proposed, yielding a...algorithm able to...
* We present a...method that deals with... In particular, given..., our method is able to...
* We approach this task with...and propose a novel...model that incorporates... The model consists of two main parts: 1)..., and 2)... Different from most competing...techniques that..., our network uses... This characteristic allows us to apply...
* We formulate the...problem over...and...jointly. The...is updated using..., while the...are updated through...
* In particular, we consider a...network under...model, in which... We derive...for... We propose a...scheme, which nearly achieves...
* First, we compute...for the proposed...scheme, based on... We also derive... Next, ...is estimated using...methods in the presence of... We highlight that...
* ...models are investigated based on...// ...are derived, which are used to...// ...is discussed, and...is used to...
* We address this issue by developing an analytical framework based on... We focus on... We analytically derive... We then investigate..., and develop... We extend... and evaluate its utility.
* Due to the diversity of..., ...are taken into account to develop... The features are designed by considering..., ..., and... The...features are then...
* Thus, with the view to enhance..., a...scheme for...in the context of...is proposed. It consists of the following two modules: 1) ..., and 2) ...

6.4 Summarizing the Research Results

In the abstract, we should also present the main results of our research. We can use the following sentence structures.

* It is shown that...can be modeled either based on...or... In addition, a...expression is obtained for...based on...
* The proposed...eliminates undesirable..., and ensures that... This approach guarantees..., and ensures that...
* The simulation results illustrate the stability of the user association and efficiency of resource allocation with higher utility gain.
* ...models with respect to...using...are provided herein, and are shown to simplify..., while allowing researchers to... A new...framework, shown to..., is presented for use in..., using...
* The performance of the proposed method is assessed using a series of experiments conducted with...and the results obtained pave the way to...
* In contrast to what has been speculated in the literature, we show that... Our results also show that...
* Results show that by jointly learning from...and..., ...improves..., which is especially obvious for..., such as... At the same time, ...improves...
* Simulation results show that our...performs closely to the optimal solution and that it significantly improves...over traditional approaches.
* By modeling...as one of the state variables, ...can be estimated, which is further corrected by...method. The...parameters from experimental results are integrated in the model, and simulation results are validated by experiment.
* The simulation results show that the proposed...approach is effective for many... scenarios, and...provides...performance and maintains good...
* It is shown that, for..., ...results in a reduction of...in...as compared to...and nearly the same...as... In addition, we show that...achieves better performance in all studied...conditions, as compared with other techniques. It is also shown to efficiently work for any configuration of...and..., even for the case of...
* Computer simulation results reveal that our...algorithm and novel...solution provide not only a superior...performance but also an increase in...compared to the ordinary... approach.
* The...of the proposed method is analyzed and numerical results confirm that the proposed scheme outperforms alternative algorithms in terms of..., while...
* Applying these methods to...has the potential to...while simultaneously improving user experience.
* Experiments in...show that...results in higher...than either of its two independent components and other state-of-the-art...

> *Results on...reveal that...outperforms...as it yields significantly more accurate affective models. Moreover, it appears that...meets and even outperforms affective models that..., for several of the scenarios examined. As the...method is...and applicable to..., the key findings of the paper suggest that...*

6.5 Presenting the Research Conclusions

We can also state the research conclusions in the abstract by using the following sentence structures.

> * *Models presented here offer side-by-side comparisons of..., and the results and models are useful for...of future...systems.*
> * *The results presented here may assist researchers in analyzing and simulating...that will rely on...*
> * *Our approach improves... It also improves state-of-the-art...performance on...*
> * *Our extensive qualitative and quantitative evaluation reveals that... Our validation also proves that..., and improves..., such as...and...*
> * *Our method is based on... This allows us to model a...that will... The method is...and the results... It outperforms the state-of-the-art...and according to several metrics, and can handle...*
> * *We evaluate the proposed approach on...and...databases as well as...database and show superior performance to state-of-the-art...and...methods. Finally, cross-database evaluation shows a high ability to..., indicating...*
> * *The proposed...model is able to...and produces convincing results for... We rigorously evaluate the proposed model on..., and report superior performance compared to the existing state-of-the-art.*
> * *Numerical results demonstrate the feasibility and performance of our approach compared to...*
> * *We prove here...and introduce...to improve... Although, we demonstrate our augmentation on...alone, in general it may be applied to any...algorithm that relies on...*
> * *Our analysis makes use of the theory of..., and develops...by... Simulation results verify our analysis, and throw up interesting open problems.*
> * *In a...study, we demonstrate its advantages and the need for... With our developed methodology, we can advance the state-of-the-art in...and provide means to...*
> * *The effectiveness of the...model is demonstrated using... The model parameters are estimated using...*

* *The contributions of this paper include: (i) an analytical model for..., (ii) the analysis of..., and (iii) the design of...*
* *The validation tests on...reveal the superior performance of the proposed approach compared to the competing metrics.*
* *Finally, the proposed scheme has been experimentally evaluated on...and...to prove its effectiveness and efficiency in terms of...and...for...*
* *To conduct realistic experiments, we made use of... Experimental results show that our proposed method significantly outperforms existing methods.*
* *The experiments show that the presented approach significantly outperforms state-of-the-art methods in...settings, both in terms of...and...*
* *Compared to state-of-the art...our...method achieves... We demonstrate its applicability to...in...and...tasks.*
* *Our experiments validate the theoretical intuitions behind our method, and we find that...achieves a comparable or better performance than..., especially on..., since it can...*
* *We describe and analyze the various improvements we applied to our own...and show the resulting performance in...*
* *We demonstrate that...can be evaluated objectively by... We find that in the evaluation practice... The analysis provides objective insight into the strengths and weaknesses of...*
* *Future trends in...are identified based on industry examples and academic research.*
* *Finally, future...strategies and functionalities in...infrastructures are addressed, and global...trends are summarized.*
* *We also discuss key challenges for future work, especially with the focus on... for...in mobile wireless networks.*

Exercises

I. Below is a random list of sentences of the abstract from a research article. Please identify the move of each sentence and determine the correct order of the sentences.

① The proposed architecture relies on a Luenberger observer together with a bank of Unknown-Intput Observers (UIOs) at each subsystem, providing attack detection capabilities.

② Our analysis shows that some classes of attacks cannot be detected using either module independently; rather, by exploiting both modules simultaneously, we are able to improve the detection properties of the diagnostic tool as a whole.

③ Theoretical results are backed up by simulations, where our method is applied to a realistic model of a low-voltage DC microgrid under attack.

④ We describe the architecture and analyze conditions under which attacks are guaranteed to be detected, and, conversely, when they are stealthy.

⑤ DC microgrids often present a hierarchical control architecture, requiring integration of communication layers.

⑥ Motivated by this application, in this paper we present a distributed monitoring scheme to provide attack-detection capabilities for linear Large-Scale Systems.

⑦ This leads to the possibility of malicious attackers disrupting the overall system.

(Gallo, A. J., Turan, M. S., Boem, F., Parisini, T. & Ferrari-Trecate, G. 2020. A distributed cyber-attack detection scheme with application to DC microgrids. *IEEE Transactions on Automatic Control*, 65(9): 3800–3815.)

Order: _____

References

Basturkmen, H. 2009. Commenting on results in published research articles and masters dissertations in Language Teaching. *Journal of English for Academic Purposes*, 8: 241–251.

Bieber, D. 1993. Representativeness in corpus design. *Literary and Linguistic Computing*, 8(4): 243–257.

Boxman, E. S. & Boxman, R. R. L. 2020. *Communicating Science: A Practical Guide for Engineers and Physical Scientists*. Beijing: Tsinghua University Press.

Coffin, C. 2009. Incorporating and evaluating voices in a film studies thesis. *Writing & Pedagogy*, 1: 163–193.

Cotos, E., Huffman, S. & Link, S. 2017. A move/step model for methods sections: Demonstrating rigour and credibility. *English for Specific Purposes*, 46: 90–106.

Glasman-Deal, H. 2009. *Science Research Writing: For Non-native English Speakers*. London: Imperial College Press.

Halliday, M. A. K. & Matthissen, M. I. M. 2014. *Halliday's Introduction to Functional Grammar* (4th ed.). New York: Routledge.

Hyland, K. 1999. Academic attribution: Citation and the construction of disciplinary knowledge. *Applied Linguistics*, 20: 341–367.

Kanoksilapatham, B. 2005. Rhetorical structure of biochemistry research articles. *English for Specific Purposes*, 24(3): 269–292.

Kanoksilapatham, B. 2015. Distinguishing textual features characterizing structural variation in research articles across three engineering sub-discipline corpora. *English for Specific Purposes*, 37: 74–86.

Mohammadi, A., Nakhkash, M. & Akhaee, M. A. 2020. A high-capacity reversible data hiding in encrypted images employing local difference predictor. *IEEE Transactions on Circuits and Systems for Video Technology*, 30(8): 2366–2376.

Pechenik, J. A. 2016. *A Short Guide to Writing about Biology* (9th ed.). Boston: Pearson.

Petric, B. 2007. Rhetorical functions of citations in high- and low-rated master's theses. *Journal of English for Academic Purposes*, *6*: 238–253.

Swales, J. M. 1990. *Genre Analysis: English in Academic and Research Settings*. London: Cambridge University Press.

Swales, J. M. & Feak, C. B. 2012. *Academic Writing for Graduate Students* (3rd ed.). Ann Arbor: University of Michigan Press.

Swales, J. M. 2014. Variation in citational practice in a corpus of student biology papers: From parenthetical plonking to intertextual storytelling. *Written Communication*, *31*: 118–141.

Toulmin, S. E. 1958. *The Uses of Argument*. Cambridge: Cambridge University Press.

Wallwork, A. 2011. *English for Writing Research Papers*. New York: Springer.

Williams, I. A. 1999. Results sections of medical research articles: Analysis of rhetorical categories for pedagogical purposes. *English for Specific Purposes*, *18*(4): 347–366.

Van Dijk, T. A. 1977. Semantic macro-structures and knowledge frames in discourse comprehension. In M. A. Just & P. A. Carpenter (Eds.), *Cognitive Processes in Comprehension*. London: Psychology Press, 332.

Zappen, J. P. 1983. A rhetoric for research in sciences and technologies. In P. V. Anderson, R. J. Brockmann & C. R. Miller (Eds.), *New Essays in Technical and Scientific Communication: Research, Theory, Practice*. London: Routledge, 123–138.

Keys to Exercises

Chapter 2 Introducing Background
I.

Excerpt	Comment
<u>Unlike the previous generation of mobile networks, 5G systems, are expected to rely on both the advancement of physical infrastructures represented by the introduction of Millimeter waves, massive MIMO, full duplex, beamforming, and small cells; as well as the emergence of SDN and NFV. By introducing the logical infrastructure abstraction, the 5G mobile networks will revamp modern network infrastructures using SDN and NFV as key enabling technologies towards softwarized networks.</u> Network Softwarization is the core concept supporting the 5G's use cases, i.e., enhanced Mobile Broadband (eMBB), Ultra-Reliable and Low Latency Communications (uRLLC), and massive Machine Type Communication (mMTC), reducing both the Capital Expenditures (CAPEX) and the OPEX of the service provider, while keeping the deployment schema simple. Network Softwarization can enable high performance improvements by offering the flexibility and modularity that are required to create multiple overlying networks. These softwarized networks' mechanisms give place to a new concept dubbed Network Slicing. Meanwhile, the Third Generation Partnership Project (3GPP), in its Releases 15 and 16, introduced a service-oriented 5G core network (5GCN) that entirely relies on NFs, which increases the need for autonomous mechanisms to deploy and manage NS through operating multiple Service Function Chains (SFC) that will dynamically steer the network traffic and flows across multiple logicaland physical infrastructures. For instance, a given userhas a network slice that consists of two SFCs:	The authors establish the research territory by claiming the centrality of 5G systems on the basis of development of physical infrastructures and the emergence of SDN and NFV. Then, they review some previous literature.

(Continued)

Excerpt	Comment
The first one is used to handle the control plane part by steering the traffic through the Access and Mobility Management Function (AMF) and the Session Management Function (SMF) which are equivalent to the MME, PDN-Gateway Control plane (P-GWCP), and Serving-Gateway Control plane (S-GWCP) in the 4G system after the control and user plane separation of EPC nodes (CUPS).	
The second SFC will ensure the reliability of the data plane by steering the data flows from the AMF to the Data Network (DN) passing by the User plane Function (UPF) which represents the P-GW User plane (P-GWUP) and the S-GW User plane (S-GWUP) in the CUPS architecture.	
As the standards development organizations (SDOs), i.e., the Next Generation Mobile Network Alliance (NGMN), 3GPP, and International Telecommunication Union Telecommunication Standardization Sector (ITU-T), are instantiating network slices that contain one or more SFCs, each SFC composed by a set of NFs running inside either a logical node or a physical node. To enable this emerging approach, many NFs may require being traversed in a certain strict order, leveraging on the flexibility of NFV, Mobile Network Operators (MNOs) can deploy any particular slice type honoring its real-time requirements. However, this flexible management can lead to a huge number of active nodes in the network infrastructure that are scarcely used, which leads to an inefficient network slicing deployment. Based on these observations, the contributions of this paper are:	The authors establish the niche with a counter-claim.
The introduction of a new architecture in compliance with the ETSI-NFV model and the 3GPP specifications to create a fine-grained NS; The formulation of a Mixed Integer Linear Programming (MILP) to achieve an efficient cross-domain network slicing deployment regardless the underlying topologies (both the VNF layer and the physical layer) while satisfying all constraints and the specifications requested by the end-users or a given vertical's application; The design and evaluation of a heuristic algorithm to overcome the exponential runtime and allow a quick decision-making capability.	Then, the niche is occupied by indicating the main contributions of the paper.
The remainder of this paper is organized as follows. Section 2 summarizes the fundamental background topics and related research works. Section 3 describes the proposed architecture and our network model. Section 4 illustrates the problem formulation and describes our proposed framework solution. Section 5 introduces the proposed heuristic for the reduction of the exponential runtime. Section 6 presents the performance evaluation and our results analysis. Finally, Section 7 concludes the paper.	Lastly, the outline of the article is stated.

Keys to Exercises

II.

1. Flexibility _always_ comes at a cost of robustness, especially when automated parameter estimation is involved.

2. It is _often_ a problem in various fields that one runs into a series of tasks that appear to be highly related to each other, yet applying the optimal machine learning solution of one problem to other results in poor performance.

3. In the context of secure control, attack detection and resilience schemes _can be often_ divided in data driven and knowledge-based approaches.

4. We test the hypothesis that DL _could_ construct feature extractors that are more appropriate than selected adhoc features picked via automatic selection.

5. Answers to this question _could_ have a major practical impact especially in those situations where identifying a process model _can be_ difficult and time consuming.

6. This difficulty has led to the proliferation of different and, _sometimes_, incompatible proposals for the practical realization of IoT systems.

7. However, acquiring these parameters _may be_ troublesome and costly.

8. Some of these agents _may be_ unreliable, and therefore the consensus process needs to be reliant.

9. An observed sequence of patterns often conveys a meaning to the observer, whereby independent fragments of this sequence _would be_ hard to decipher in isolation.

10. Assuming robust deep learning is achieved, it _would be_ possible to train such a hierarchical network on a large set of observations and later extract signals from this network to a relatively simple classification engine for the purpose of robust pattern recognition.

III.

1. In statistics and data analysis, one typically proceeds from data presented in the form of real numbers or categorical values, implicitly assuming the underlying measurement process to be precise and exact. In many cases, however, this _assumption_ is clearly not warranted.

2. We shall now introduce three categories of prediction problems, all of key relevance to the operations and management of commercial mobile wireless networks. This _categorization_ is

not meant to be exhaustive, although vast majority of problems we have encountered fall into one of these categories.

3. Many machine learning techniques are tied to a series of hyper-parameters and/or selection of sub-components that need to be tuned. This *challenge* can broadly be defined as the algorithm configuration problem.

4. In the context of formation control, most of the proposed approaches are based on the notion of navigation function, which is constructed from the geometric information on the considered topology and then employed to define gradient descent control laws. This *concept* has been recently extended to the multi-agent scenario, both in a centralized and decentralized implementation.

5. Any successful attack on CPS may jeopardize critical infrastructure and people's lives and properties, even threaten national security. In 2010, Stuxnet malware launched a devastating attack on Iranian uranium enrichment facilities. This *incident* raised a great deal of attention to CPS security in recent years.

6. Although there is not yet a formal and widely accepted definition of "Smart City", the final aim is to make a better use of the public resources, increasing the quality of the services offered to the citizens, while reducing the operational costs of the public administrations. This *objective* can be pursued by the deployment of an urban IoT.

7. During the first three decades of research, the fuzzy logic community has more focused on topics in the realm of knowledge and information processing, such as control and approximate reasoning, and less on analyzing and learning from data. This *focus* started to change in the recent past, which has been characterized by a shift from largely knowledge-based to strongly data-driven fuzzy modeling.

8. Comprehensibility was defined as the learning algorithm ability for encoding its model in such a way that it may be inspected and understood by humans. This *definition* narrows the focus to the model itself.

9. Baseline PI is extended to include an appropriate combination of PI task selection and soft-max task selection. This *development* improves performance and boosts the exploratory properties of the algorithm, meaning that escape from local minima is possible.

10. We define a matrix-valued function, for each agent, which is similar in spirit to the definition of a standard navigation function. This *function* is modified by the presence of

additional dynamics and the resulting value functions are smooth, hence yielding smooth control laws.

IV.

1. The application of the IoT paradigm to the Smart City is particularly attractive to local and regional administrations that may become the early adopters of such technologies, *thus acting* as catalyzers for the adoption of the IoT paradigm on a wider scale.

2. These two modules exploit different sets of relations and different model knowledge to perform detection, *thus compensating* each other's vulnerabilities, and reducing the number of attacks that are stealthy.

3. Recent neuroscience findings have provided insight into the principles governing information representation in the mammalian brain, *leading to* new ideas for designing systems that represent information.

4. In the past, these systems were standalone and isolated from the world, *making* them unsusceptible to external malicious attacks.

5. A blockchain contains a set of blocks, and every block contains a hash of the previous block, *creating* a chain of blocks from the genesis block to the current block.

6. To the best of the authors' knowledge, this is the first-time deep learning is introduced to the domain of psychophysiology, *yielding* efficient computational models of affect.

7. A simultaneous proliferation of high-value connected devices makes the IoT a desirable attack surface, and drives security-related resource requirements, *demanding* high-powered computation—lest a platform become unfavorable for mission-critical applications.

8. They successfully managed to learn decoding rules with high accuracy using only a fraction of the training trials required by the earlier approaches, *allowing* subjects to communicate consistently with a computer in a single session.

9. The study compares DL against ad-hoc feature extraction on physiological signals, used broadly in the AC literature, *showing* that DL yields models of equal or significantly higher accuracy when a single signal is used as model input.

10. Batches of random experiences are drawn from the buffer and used for updates, *forcing* the network to generalize beyond what it is currently doing in the environment.

Chapter 3 Describing Methods

I.

Excerpt	Comment
Fig. 1 depicts the architecture overview suggested in this paper. We have divided the architecture into three layers, as it integrates the ETSI-NFV model and the 3GPP entities to enable the monitoring, selection and creation process of the virtual instances. The physical layer consists of a set of servers and routers. In this layer, the servers are grouped into a set of data centers that communicate between themselves through the physical network. A set of routers would be used as connectors for connecting different data centers. In the NFV model, this layer refers to the NFV infrastructure (NFVI) and would be controlled by the Virtualized Infrastructure Manager (VIM) presented in the same figure. The VNF layer consists of a set of virtual network functions (VNFs) created on top of the servers. Each VNF is dedicated to one or many functionalities during the forwarding of different data traffics. The VNF layer is managed by the VNF Manager (VNFM) that ensures the life-cycle management of all VNF instances spreading over multiple administrative domains. The slice layer, which runs on top of the VNF layer, consists of a set of slices that are dedicated to different services, e.g., health-care and connected cars. The traffic in each slice is routed thanks to service function chaining (SFC), where each traffic in the slice would be forwarded using a predefined order. Each slice is formed by ingress, egress nodes, as well as a set of intermediate nodes. At the reception of different packets at the ingress node, which is also called classifier, the SFC of those packets would be identified, and then the traffic would be forwarded according to that specified SFC. <u>It is noticed that the AMF is considered the classifier in the 3GPP standardization as it is the shared entity between the control plane and the data plane. For instance, in the case of connected car management that belong to the URLLC category, a slice can be comprised of more than one SFC inside a given network infrastructure. While the first SFC could be dedicated to the monitoring and control plane information, the second SFC could be used for applying different management actions i.e., the data plane. In the following work, only the core network, (CN) part is considered, while the radio part was not studied. However, the proposed solution can be also used to deploy RAN slices or RAN/CN slices if the RAN part is an NF on top of the cloud/data-center.</u>	The first sentence presents an overview of the principle by which the model works. Then, the authors briefly describe the principal parts of the figure. Lastly, the underlined sentences explain how the figure works.

II.

Excerpt	Comment
<u>In this section the desired evolution of the disturbance-free model (5) will be obtained with the use of a reaching law-based control strategy.</u> In particular, we used a generalization of Gao's seminal reaching law for the case of relative degree two sliding variables since such a strategy has been shown to provide better dynamical properties of the system than its relative degree one equivalent [32]. The considered reaching law is expressed in the following way(12) where $s_m(k)$ is the relative degree two sliding variable (8) $\varepsilon>0$, $1>q>0$ and are the design parameters. The objective of this strategy is to drive the system representative point to an arrow vicinity of the sliding hyperplane and to ensure that the hyperplane is crossed in each step. We obtain the control signal which satisfies these properties by substituting (10) into the left hand side of reaching law (12) and solving the obtained equation for $u_m(k)$. Then, the control signal has the following form (13). In formerly published literature [32] several advantageous properties of reaching law (12) have been proven. Two of those properties will now be quoted.	In the beginning of this section, the authors state the purpose of the method. Then they briefly review previous work, which serves as theoretical basis of the method. Lastly, they explain how their strategy works in detail.

Chapter 4 Reporting Results

I.

Excerpt 1	Comment
We train and test our system on a PC with an Intel Core i7-6700 k CPU, 16 GB RAM, and one Nvidia GTX 1080 graphics card with 8 GB memory. The average time cost of each training iteration is 0.25 s on GPU, and it takes 1.4 hours for 20,000 iterations to complete the whole training process. Given a reasonably large mesh from the SCAPE dataset (12,500 vertices, 24,998 triangles), it takes 26.4 s to compute the raw SH descriptors from the mesh on CPU, 0.09 s to compute the distance metric on GPU, 0.06 s to compute the saliency map on GPU, and 163.4 s to compute 30 saliency-induced embeddings from the metric on CPU. The method of [25] takes about 235.2 s for shape matching on CPU.	The authors refer back to the methodology by adding details of the apparatus and parameters, in order to help that are important for readers to re-generate the experiment.

(Continued)

Excerpt 2	Comment
The visual quality of classical images and videos is generally measured by a global quality index that (ideally) integrates all the possible sources of distortion into a single or a few values. However, as aforementioned, the sources of distortions in 360-degree videos are numerous and quite different, and their combination into a global index is far from trivial.	The authors contextualize the results by providing background information about the method used.
Table II summarizes the different types of distortions commonly found in 360-degree video. We broadly categorize them as: *spatial*, i.e., those related to still image compression and can appear in both images and videos; *temporal*, i.e., those related to the temporal evolution of images and appear only on video; *stereoscopic*, i.e., those related to binocular vision; and *navigation*, i.e., those that only appear while the user navigates through the scene.	Then, they report the results with a table, and describe the main categories of results in the table.
The ultimate way to assess the 360-degree visual quality is through subjective tests. Such tests, however, are time consuming and expensive. Thus, objective metrics have been proposed for omnidirectional video in the past few years. However, it is quite challenging to capture all the effects that impact the QoE of 360-degree videos, and much work remains to be done in this area, in particular, with regards to perceptually optimized metrics.	After summarizing the main results, the authors point out a direction for further research.

II.

Excerpt	Comment
① Table VII summarizes metadata for experiment set A using row communication, and Tables VIII and IX repeat these statistics for mesh and hybrid communication. ② In these tables, σ is the percentage improvement of the soft-max variant when compared to the solution generated by the baseline, and θ is the number of additional problems that each algorithm could solve (i.e., the number unsolvable by the baseline but solvable by the algorithm in question). ③ In calculating the percentage of problems solved, the number of problems was taken as 32, as 4 problems could not be solved by any method in any of the tests. ④ The data are also	Sentence ① is a summary statement about the table. Sentences ② highlights the parameters in the table. Sentence ③ provides some supplementary information about the results in the table, followed by a reference to Figure 4 for details.

Keys to Exercises

(Continued)

Excerpt	Comment
depicted as a bar chart in Fig. 4 for ease of comparison. ⑤ Note that if the sum of the percentages of best solutions is greater than 100% it is because two algorithms generated the same best solution.	Sentence ⑤ explains how some numbers are obtained in the table.

III.

Excerpt 1

As shown in Fig. 11, in general, the users' throughput <u>decreases</u> when the number of Wi-Fi channels is reduced. Among all the methods, the performance of the SSS <u>decreases</u> the most significantly. This is because the SSS assigns users to Wi-Fi regardless of its capacity and availability. Thus, when the Wi-Fi capacity is <u>reduced</u>, the performance of those Wi-Fi users is severely <u>compromised</u>. Unlike the SSS, the other methods have the ability to balance the loads between Li-Fi and Wi-Fi, and thus are less <u>affected</u> by a reduced number of Wi-Fi channels. In addition, as the number of Wi-Fi channels <u>increases</u>, the performance of the FL-SSS gradually <u>approaches</u> that of the FL-LB. The reason for this trend is that when more users are migrated to Wi-Fi, the gap between using the LB and SSS in Li-Fi becomes <u>smaller</u>.

Excerpt 2

Fig. 9 presents the users' satisfaction and fairness of various methods when the average required data rate is 10 Mbps. As shown in Fig. 9(a), the proposed method can significantly <u>increase</u> the users' satisfaction over the SSS and LB, especially for a large number of users. When 30 users are present, using the SSS can meet the data requirements for only 74.6% of the users. This value is <u>increased to</u> 87.4% by employing the LB instead of the SSS. When using the FL-SSS and FL-LB, the proportion of satisfied users is 96.1% and 91.9%, respectively. Note that there is <u>across point</u> between the curves of the FL-SSS and FL-LB. This is because using the LB in the proposed method can <u>improve</u> the performance of deeply-unsatisfied users, by <u>decreasing</u> the number of satisfied users. In Fig. 9(b), the fairness among users is shown for different numbers of users. Two outcomes are observed: i) the fairness of all methods equals 1 given a small number of users; ii) as the number of users increases, the fairness <u>decreases</u> for all methods, but the fairness of the FL-LB decreases much <u>slower</u> than that of the other methods. At the fairness of the FL-LB <u>achieves</u> 0.95, while the remaining methods have a fairness below 0.9.

Chapter 5 Discussing Findings

I.

1. Taking inspiration from OMP, we *could* reduce potential error accumulation in the estimated nk by recalculating all of their values upon each successive detection of a fluorescent emitter.

2. Our super-resolution imaging method *can be* applied to a wider variety of applications that employ forward models.

3. Each node *might* publish its own features and data by running a CoAP server, though this feature is not yet implemented in the testbed.

4. The proxy logic *can be extended* to better support monitoring applications and limit the amount of traffic injected into the IoT peripheral network.

5. Examining the readings of the other sensors in the same time interval, we *can* note a sharp decrease of light intensity and temperature, and an increase in humidity.

6. Several applications with different performance requirements *may* require access to the same piece of information at the same time.

7. The reduction in resource requirements *would* allow sensing and connectivity to migrate into very low-power wearable devices, reducing the cost and complexity of contemporary health-aware clothing

8. When the target appearance changes gradually the prediction *is more likely to* succeed.

9. *It is likely that* all the methods presented here would perform better if prior knowledge had been incorporated into choosing the feature space.

10. In passive (data-only) systems, sensors *can* fail, connections *can* drop, or a proxy's model *might be proven* inaccurate or incomplete.

II.

1. *Since* the IoT devices could be part of different management domains during their lifetimes, that information would be spread among many nodes making it difficult to audit and track it.

2. Public lighting operators will be equipped with mobile devices that can locate the streetlight that requires intervention, issue actuation commands directly to the IoT node connected to the lamp, and signal the result of the intervention to the central system that can track every

single lamppost and, *hence*, optimize the maintenance plan.

3. The SPC cannot cope with the concept change within a user *because* it does not have any mechanism to forget old records.

4. The work represents an important extension to the baseline as real missions take place in dynamically changing environments where the SA is subject to alter rapidly. Task allocation strategies must *therefore* be able to adjust to new data and recompute new solutions in real time.

5. It is possible to specify a list of resources that need to be monitored, *so that* the server can autonomously update the entries in a cache related to those devices.

6. An approach based on hierarchical reinforcement learning (HRL) was chosen, *as* it is a promising approach to expand traditional RL methods to work with more difficult and complex tasks.

Chapter 6 Writing Abstract

Lead-in

Sentences 1 and 2 introduce the research background. Sentences 3, 4 and 5 state the purpose of the research. Sentences 6, 7 and 8 describe the methods of the research. Sentence 9 shows the results, and Sentence 10 discusses the results.

Exercises

Order: ⑤ ⑦ ⑥ ① ④ ② ③

Sentences ⑤ and ⑦ indicate the research background. Sentence ⑥ presents the purpose of the research. Sentences ① and ④ describe the research method. Sentence ② shows the research results. Sentence ③ presents the research conclusion.